A New You

Life's Revitalization

A New You

Life's Revitalization

Carrie R. Gramling

iUniverse, Inc.
New York   Bloomington

iUniverse books may be ordered through booksellers or by contacting:

iUniverse
1663 Liberty Drive
Bloomington, IN 47403
www.iuniverse.com
1-800-Authors (1-800-288-4677)

Because of the dynamic nature of the Internet, any Web addresses or links contained in this book may have changed since publication and may no longer be valid. The views expressed in this work are solely those of the author and do not necessarily reflect the views of the publisher, and the publisher hereby disclaims any responsibility for them.

ISBN: 978-1-4401-3315-2 (sc)
ISBN: 978-1-4401-3314-5 (ebook)

Printed in the United States of America

iUniverse rev. date: 05/04/2009

*This book is dedicated to the memory of
Willis Reed Gramling, my mother*

And

Tessie Mae Brown, my aunt

My two guardian angels

"You are missed very much"

Thanks

I want to give thanks to my Lord and Savior Jesus Christ. I want to give a lot of thanks to my mother; Willis Reed Gramling (God rest her soul) for being a strong mother figure, and pushing me to be strong willed, positive, independent and has morals and values for myself. I would like to give a lot of thanks to you, Aunt Tessie, (God rest her soul) for being yourself and having your direct, critical and independent attitude.

I want to give thanks to my whole family for being there when I needed any of them; I love you all very much.

A special thanks to my brother, Lester Gramling Jr. thank you for always being there for me anytime I needed you, and thanks for instilling very wise business sense into me, I love you very much. And my sister Lola A. Pemberton thanks for always being there for me. Thanks for listening to anything I had to talk about. Thanks for making it possible for me to be myself in my younger years. I love you very much. I want to give a lot of thanks to my baby sister Barbara A. Gramling, for sharing her thoughts, listening to me at all times, believing in me, giving me corrective criticism and all those late night wake up calls, just to ask her opinion on anything, thank you Brady for being there and for being so patient, love you. And thanks to my nephew Michael A. Gramling for being so real about anything I ask him especially about an opinion about a male person's roll.

I would like to thank my two beautiful girls, Tamira J. Biggers and Talonda I. Johnson. Thank you God, for bringing them into my life. Girls you have brought great things into my life, I can't think of words to express the way I feel. The way you two are always there for me. The respect you two show for yourselves and me. You two have grown up to be perfect, successful young ladies; and a very big inspiration to me. Tammy thanks for my two beautiful grandchildren, Antonio Dewann Biggers Jr. and Jaylen Darnell Biggers. Tammy always thank God for blessing you with a very good soul mate (husband) Antonio Dewann Biggers Sr. Thanks Dawann for making my child happy. Toy continue to reach for your goal in life, the sky is the limit.

In the absence of my mother Willis Reed Gramling and my aunt Tessie Mae Brown, I present this book to my two girls, Tamira J. Biggers and Talonda I. Johnson, to accept this book in memory of Mama and Aunt Tessie.

Love You All,

Carrie R. Gramling

Prelude

"Good morning Mary." " Good morning John you're up and dressed awfully early this morning. Is anything wrong? Are you alright?" " Mary nothing's wrong, I'm alright. I just have something on my mind. I've been up and down all night. When I saw the sun come up I just got up, took my shower and got dressed." " Oh yea! It's some sausage, bacon and toast on the stove. I made some coffee also. You want me to fix you some grits and eggs?" "No honey," said Mary. " I'll fix it, you come in the kitchen with me and let's talk about what's on your mind. They walk in the kitchen very slowly, Mary leading him by the hand and looking up at him with a very concerned look on her face. Mary knew her husband very well. His behavior was very strange but yet familiar. His face was pale like all the blood had left. His eyes had the look of confusion in them. His actions brought back memories of when John was called to preach the gospel, which was twenty years ago.

Mary went with him down at the kitchen table. She got two cups, sugar, cream, pot of coffee and a spoon. She sat them on the table then sat down across from John. She asked him if he would like to share what was on his mind. John's eyes looked like he was staring straight through her. His eyes were roaming back and forth like he could see a vision of what was on his mind. He said, " Mary you remember the few times this week I told you I had been riding around in different neighborhoods on the south side of town? It seemed like a force was pushing me in that area of town.

When I got to York Street the force lead me down it. I got in front of this store, a voice told me you are here study it. I looked around, I saw young girls and boys standing on the streets with beer, wine and God knows what else. All kinds of language were coming from their mouths. The third day I rode through there I stopped because I saw this young lady standing beside the news stand in front of the store. The look on her face said, " Help please." I got out of the car and walked over to her. I asked, " Young lady are you alright? " She said, " No sir, I don't have nowhere to go, my mama and daddy put me out because I use crack. They got my little girl and won't let me see her. I tried to tell them, I quit using but they don't believe me because I done told so many lies." I asked her if she was still using crack. She said, " Yes," but she didn't want to, she just couldn't stop." I also talked to some more boys and girls. Mary those kids are drunks, drug dealers, crack addicts, and prostitutes. You name it they are out there. Some of them seem to be very intelligent. They are lost and reaching out for help. The Lord has lead me to them. It's some members in the church that have gone astray.

I had to pray and ask God to show me how to handle those lost souls. I've been thinking very hard about putting together some kind of program to win lost souls. Mary I don't want to run them farther into the world I want them to trust me. Mary stood up walked around the table stood behind John she said, " John honey turn and look at me." He turned and looked at her. She puts her hands on his shoulders, looked him in his eyes and said, " John you are the chosen one from the Lord. The Lord has chosen you to lead these people to him. He has already prepared you to do it. All you have to do is put the plan to work. John be obedient, I am behind you one hundred percent."

CHAPTER ONE

Mary, Reverend Franks called," I'm going in the study to prepare for the church meeting on this evening." He walks up to her gives her a big hug and a small kiss on the forehead, he looks down at her, she looks up at him, the vibes coming from her husband's eyes was saying, thanks for loving, trusting, understanding, standing by and believing in me. Reverend John Franks was a man determined to be obedient to the Lord and bring the worldly people into the light of God. Mary Franks is Reverend John Franks' wife; she is very supportive of her husband. John said," I thank God everyday for you." Mary smiles at him and replies," John we are as one, to death do we part, now you go in the study and get your meeting in order, I'm fixing us something so we can eat before the meeting okay". John replied," okay dear". Mary finished their meal and they ate.

When John and Mary arrived at the church a half hour early, Deacon Smith was already there. (Deacon Robert Smith is a deacon in Mount Sinai Baptist Church, Reverend John Frank's church. Deacon Smith is a good Christian man who is faithful to the church and Reverend Frank's right hand man). He fears God and wants to make sure he does things right and is very obedient to God. " Deacon Smith is here, that is one dependable man," said Mary. "Yes, I can always depend on him," said John. Reverend Franks pulled into his parking space marked pastors parking. He stopped the car, got out, went around the car and opened the passenger's side to assist Mary getting out of the car.

As they walked to the front door of the church. Mary said," Oh yea! John while I'm thinking about it you see those trees over there; Mary pointed at the trees, they either need to be trimmed or cut down, because they are about to reach those lines, when bad weather gets here those limbs could break the lines. Those floral arrangements at the front entrance of the church need to be changed if you want me to I would be glad to change it. Sure Mary, it would be all right for you to change those flowers. Sister Williams use to keep them up, but since she started working her time is limited with her taking care of her family and all.

Here comes Sister Lily, Sister Dot and Brother Bill. Mary I better get in there and get set up. I need to get some things out of the office, and say a little something to Deacon Smith. If I get stuck out here talking to Brother Bill I will never get in the church, come on honey. Deacon Smith meets them at the door of the church; "Good evening Deacon," said Reverend Franks. "Good evening Reverend and Mrs. Franks." Deacon I need you to come with me to my office. Mary will you set up my table for the meeting, then come on back to the office and I will give you those papers I need recorded for tomorrow said Reverend Franks. Okay John, don't let me forget to get that disc out of the computer, oh that's all right I need to do something on this computer before I leave that's what I came for. She puts her hand to her mouth and laughs. Reverend Franks tells Deacon Smith, and Brother Thomas to start the meeting. Deacon Smith states," the main purpose of this meeting is to collect the $500.00 from each organization in the church and brief them on what the money will be used for, right" Yes Deacon, here's some notes that I wrote down that might help you. I will be in there in a few minutes; I have something I need to share with you all. "Okay Reverend, I'll see you when you get in there," replied Deacon Smith.

Reverend Franks sat in his office praying and meditating. He got up from his desk and joined the meeting. Deacon Smith turned the meeting over to Reverend Franks. Reverend Franks stood and went to the podium. Good evening everyone, it is so good to see everyone at this meeting. Does everyone understand what Deacon Smith shared with you all? Are there any questions? All the members replied, "No". Since there are no questions we will close this part of the meeting. I have something else I would like to share with you all. There is a project that I want you all to work on with me. This project can help the church as well as others. I have been riding around in different neighborhoods observing the different life styles a lot of people live including children. I have spoken with some of them. One young lady told me she lives on the streets because her parents put her out of the house because she was on crack cocaine. But now she sees why they did it. She said she wants to stop using but she just can't. I spoke with some drunks, drug dealers and a number of others out there. These people are humans and some are very intelligent. So let us go out of our way to minister to them and try to get them to give their lives to God and let God handle their problems.

Sister Lily Mae Johnson spoke up and said, "Reverend you mean to tell me you been going out in the streets in those low life neighborhoods by yourself? All kinds of people that do any and everything are out there. You can get killed out there. My sister's son sales that dope or use's it one. Every time you turn around he's in jail or in some kind of trouble. I told my sister I'll pray for him, but he won't get no more of my money. Sister Lily Mae Johnson is a hypocrite who loves to brag on something she does in or away from the church. Deacon Smith spoke up," Reverend what you're talking about I believe it's a lost cause. A lot of them have come up to me asking me for money, they would lie and say it was for one thing them go buy dope, beer or liquor. I would talk to them, and invite them to church they would say okay and I wouldn't see them again." Brother Billy Moore a False Prophet who wanted to control the message from God spoke up, "Reverend I know what you're talking about". He stood up walked to the front where Reverend Franks was standing. I go out there all the time and minister to those people of all ages. I tell them the life they're living is not right. I have been there" and done that" and that I have changed my life myself and I can help change theirs. I know I can do it I tell them. Brother Bill starts jumping around shouting and hollering; I can make them walk right, I can make them talk right, and I can turn their life around. Sister Lily spoke up," Reverend you know the prayers I pray will reach those poor souls."

Reverend Franks spoke up; if anyone sees Brother Bob please fill him in on this meeting. He called me this evening; he's out of town and couldn't make it to this meeting, he's in Delaware visiting his people. Sister Mae a backbiter that loves to find out everyone's business and gossip about it, also Sister Lily's sister who thinks the choir can't do without her beautiful voice spoke up, "Well Reverend Brother Bob must have caught a jet back here, because I just seen his lying butt on my way here to church. He was turning going down in Tank Town. You know you can get any and everything in Tank Town. But I know I will see him and will sure tell him. Sister Dot, Sister Dorothy Jean Mints who's an adulterer and does any and everything she can to try and seduce Reverend Franks spoke up, You mean Reverend Brother Bob who don't never make it to these meetings every since he was put as treasurer of the Stewart board, well Reverend I would be glad to help you with those books when your wife is busy doing something else. That's good to know Sister Dot said Reverend Franks. If there's no more business to discuss let's stand and have a word of prayer before we dismiss. Everybody bow your heads:

Dear Heavenly Father we thank you for your son Jesus, Lord thank you for the members that took time from their busy schedule to attend this meeting. Lord bless each and everyone of them. Lord be with them on there way home protect them on the highways, Lord let this meeting be help to each and everyone that was spoken about here tonight. Lord help our plan to be a success. Lord we give you the glory and the praise A-men. Everybody keep those souls in your prayers. Goodnight everybody.

Reverend Franks disappeared to the back of the church. He was so ready to get away from the negative surroundings he was feeling. Every step he took he was reliving the positive conversation he and his wife had earlier that evening. He kept hearing over and over in his mind; John be obedient. A smile came up on his face, because he knew it was the Lord speaking in his wife's voice. While Reverend Franks was gathering his belongings from his office to exit the church to go home, the phone rang. He reached and picked the receiver up, answering in a very calm and collecting voice; Hello Mount Sinai Baptist Church, Reverend John Franks speaking. "Hi Reverend Franks," this is Florence Jones, Brother Bob's wife. Sister Flo is Brother Bob's wife who's a God fearing woman and lives everyday on faith and loves her family very much. I called to your home; Sister Mary told me I might catch you before you leave the church I hope I am not bothering you. "Sister Flo you're not bothering me it's always good to hear from you. How are you doing on this fine Saturday evening", said Reverend Franks. I'm doing just fine. My reason for calling is I have the $500.00 that Bob owes from the Stewart board. I said to myself I better get that money to the church for him. I would've brought it to the meeting but I had to fix the children some supper. "Sister I can understand that, I thought you all were in Delaware?" Sister Flo paused for a while; Reverend," is that what Bob told you?" Reverend, I really need to talk to somebody, may I share something with you, I can bring the money to the church right now. "Yes sister, I would love to hear what you have to share. I tell you what; I was getting ready to go home when you called its closer for you to come by my home. Give me about 10 to 15 minutes and come on by, okay! See you then bye-bye. "Alright Reverend," said sister Flo.

Deacon Smith walked up to Brother Bill with a very concerned serious look on his face. "Brother Bill, can I talk to you a minute, sure Deacon what is it," asked Brother Bill. Reverend Franks is very serious about those people out in the streets. I hope I didn't offend him by what I said. "Those people have to want help, they got to want to change their lives." Brother Bill said with a very convincing tone in his voice," Deacon just like I said in the meeting I go out there and talk to a lot of those people, I know I can lead them. I tell them the things they need to know and the things they need to do. I'm going to call Reverend tonight, when I get home and tell him don't worry I'll handle this project." Deacon Smith smiled and patted Brother Bill on the back, as he starts to walk off he turned and replied okay Brother Bill you handle it. I'm going to call Reverend Franks also. I don't want him to think I'm against what he wants to do. He doesn't need to be going out there by himself anymore. I'm very concerned about his safety. Those people can't be helped unless they want help. Deacon Smith continues to lock up as Brother Bill leaves the church. Sister Lily walks up to Deacon Smith, "Deacon I overheard you talking to Brother Bill, you know he thinks he's more powerful than God." Deacon you know for yourself my prayers are very powerful. I'll get on my street corner and pray a prayer so loud the whole neighborhood will hear me. You know prayers can travel all the way over to china. Ain't no way I'm going in that demon infested neighborhood. Never nobody hit me cross the head, rob and kill me.

Sister Dot walked by saying to everybody" Well y'all I got to go cause I got to make a stop before I get home. You know my old man's out of town. That makes me home alone. See y'all!" Sister Mae walked toward the door saying, "Lily if you're coming you better come on, you know I'm on a mission, wait Mae! "Deacon I'll see you," yelled out Sister Lily rushing toward Sister Mae. Lily did you hear Sister Dot? Yea she got to make a stop all right, to meet somebody's husband. You here that remark she made in the meeting to Reverend Franks. Sister Mary better watch out cause she's after Reverend real hard. Mae you need to shut up. The Reverend ain't like that. He got other thangs on his mind other than thinking about committing adultery. Sister Lily turned, Deacon, let me know what the outcome is on Reverend Frank's project. I got to go home and take these shoes off and rest my poor aching feet and legs I have been on them all day helping folks and listening to their problems. Come on Mae, if you'd get you some from somebody's son, you probably wouldn't be talking about folks all the time. Sister Mae walked fast behind Sister Lily; Lily slow down, don't walk so fast. Girl I got to go find Brother Bob and see why he lied to Reverend Franks, saying he was out of town, she turned and asked," are you coming Deacon?" Sister Lily looked at Sister Mae and said Ya see Mae you fixing to get all up in somebody's business. Deacon Smith locking the church doors, "yes I'm right behind you all; got to make sure I lock up good."

CHAPTER TWO

Reverend Franks walk into his living room, and flops down on his sofa. He sits there very quiet in very deep meditation. Mary comes in from the kitchen, she sees him sitting there. Hi! John, I didn't hear you come in. How was the meeting? John looks at Mary, shaking his head, he lifts his hands and says: I don't know. Mary sits on the sofa beside him, she puts her hand on his leg, she calls his name very softly, John", John" no one said this was going to be easy. It's not going to happen overnight. But Mary", they are very intelligent people. They don't want to be out there. The Lord has laid it on my heart to "lead them to him", "to help them to have faith in him", "to rescue them from those hands". Like Daniel says; God will rescue you from the devils hands Daniel 3:17. Like in Hebrews 11:34 I have to teach them to believe and turn their weakness into strength like Shad rack, Meshack and Abed ego in the fiery furnace.

Mary it seems like people have forgotten the meaning of missionary and Christian. Missionary means: concerned with religious missions. "Lord knows this is a religious mission". Christian means: Christ's teaching; believing in or following the religion of Christ, and showing compassionate qualities. I shared this project with my members tonight. They didn't show any kind of compassion. In so many words they were saying there's no help for the people out there, and in so many word they are saying I am crazy for going in that neighborhood. Brother Bill said he could handle the project himself. Brother Bill wants to control God's plan, which he can't because he's weak. He's all about self. My members have forgotten all about missionary. All they want to do is hide behind doors and walls. They have forgotten where they came from and how they got where they are. Your members are scared, Mary spoke up: John just because your members are negative against it; that means their faith and belief is weak in God. Don't let them discourage you. John you follow your heart and be obedient to God okay!

Oh yea! Deacon Smith and Brother Bill called for you; they said they would call later. Reverend Franks gets up heads toward the study; he turns around: Oh Mary! Sister Flo is coming by tonight; when she get here send her to my study. Okay! Said Mary. John goes into the study and shuts the door. The doorbell rings; Mary answers the door, hi! Sister Flo, how are you doing tonight? I'm doing fine and you? Asked Sister Flo. How're the children doing? Asked Mary. They're fine, bad as ever. Sister Flo John is waiting for you in his study. Come on its right back here. Mary opens the door; John here's Sister Flo. Come on in Sister" said Reverend Franks, he gets up from his desk, extends his hand out and shakes her hand, have a seat right here and make yourself comfortable. He walks over and shuts the door; walks back over to his desk and sits down. Okay Sister what may I help you with? Said Reverend Franks. Sister Flo sits back in her chair holds her head down looking at her hands in her lap; she looks up at Reverend Franks and says: Reverend Bob has strayed away from his family, church and everything. I know he has not paid the $500.00 for the Stewart board, the dead line is tomorrow. That's why I called you so I could pay it. Reverend, Bob has spent that money somewhere out in the streets. If I don't pay this money it would be hard for me to hold my head up in church. You know Sister Mae would tell everybody. So Sister, Brother Bob was lying when he called me and said he was out of town? Reverend Bob don't have relatives or friends in Delaware. See Reverend, that's what I'm talking about. He is a liar. He tells me he's at all kind of church meetings with you. Like tonight he told me he was going to the meeting. He was suppose to have gotten our neighbors daughter to sit with the kids until I got home from work. I called Sue before I left for work this morning and asked her if she would keep check on my children for me until I get off work. I shouldn't have to do that because I have a husband, we should work together. His money don't make it home anymore. We have bills that are behind. We don't talk anymore. He's a different person. (Sister Flo starts crying) Reverend I believe he's seeing another woman, doing drugs and God knows what else. I am so scared. He told me a couple months ago that he was going out with this guy he works with named Jim. Since then he started changing. I pray every day for my husband to come back to me. I don't like this sneaky secretive person he has become. I keep giving him to God and snatching him back, thinking I can bring him back to reality. It seems like the more I do and the more I say it pushes him farther away. Reverend, I am hurt, confused and tired of being tired. I am not going to turn my back on my family I still love Bob very much. I am giving him to the Lord and leaving him there this time and let the Lord deal with him. Sister Flo, I'm so sorry that negative spirit has gotten in your home. You see sister, the devil never sleeps; he's on call twenty-four hours a day. Whenever he sees the least little crack he can crawl into he will. Brother Bob let his guard down so the devil intervenes. Believe me; Brother Bob is just as scared, ashamed and confused as you are. He has allowed himself to get into that situation. So he has to wake up and get himself out or lose everything and let the devil claim victory. Sister Flo, you continue to stay prayed up. The devil's going to keep messing with you; rebuke him in the name of the father, the son and the Holy Spirit. You anoint yourself, your children, your car, your home and everything you can think of. Just put everything in God's hands and leave it. Reverend Franks, I am so scared that things could never be the way they use to be between Bob and I. I don't know if I could ever trust him again said Sister Flo with her head hanging down. Sister! Sister Flo! Reverend Franks calls her name: Pray; God does miracles. Come on Sister Flo let's pray: He gets some anointing oil and anoints her forehead.

Dear heavenly father I thank you so very much for your son Jesus: Lord I thank you for my life, health and strength: Lord I hold up to you Sister Flo and her family; Lord she has come to me with a burdened down heart: Her mind is confused: She feels ashamed: She's tried to fix it herself Lord: Let her know it's beyond her fixing: It's something only you can do: Lord tap Brother Bob on the shoulder, get his attention and tell him he has a beautiful family at home that love him very much, and that they need him. Remind him that the devil don't love him, he just love company. Lord touch the children let them know their daddy will be back in a little while, because Lord this is just a test. Lord direct Sister Flo in the right direction, keep her strong, and Lord instill in her wisdom and meaning. This is my prayer A-men

Now Sister you go home and give those beautiful children a kiss and hug. Your problem is fixed. You know the Lord is right on time. Thank You Reverend said Sister Flo. You're always welcome. Sister Flo leaves and goes home.

Brother Bob pulls his car in the driveway, parks and gets out. He starts walking up the street, a car pulls up and stops *(Brother Bob is a very big liar about anything especially to his wife.)* a voice calls out; Brother Bob! Brother Bob! He stops, turns around and looks at the car. The door opens and the person gets out. Hi Brother Bob how are you this fine evening? Hi Sister Mae is that you? With a surprised look on his face. Yes it's me said Sister Mae. What a surprise! What brings you this way? Said Brother Bob. You weren't at the meeting tonight. The Reverend said you called him and said you were out of town. I know I saw you on my way to church for the meeting tonight. I just want to know why did you lie to the Reverend. Reverend Franks he's the one lying. I didn't call and tell him that I was out of town. I don't know why people want to lie on me. I didn't make the meeting because I had something very important to take care of and had to do it the same time the meeting was scheduled, said Brother Bob. Sister Mae puts her hands on her hips and walks closer to Brother Bob and says; so you mean to tell me, down in Tank Town was more important than the meeting, because that's where I saw you going. You know anything down there ain't no good. They need to name it Bad News Town. Brother Bob turns and starts walking down the street toward his house; Sister Mae follows behind ,him he spins around and says: Yes you saw me go down into Tank Town. I was trying to find this guy named Jim, I work with him. He and his wife are having problems. I have been talking and spending time with him, trying to get him to give his life to God. I know he hangs down in Tank Town. I just went to see if I saw him. Brother Bob! Do I look like I got stupid wrote across my forehead? I know Jim and I know his wife. Jim ain't no good, but he got a good wife she's so sweet. I don't see what she wants with him. He does her like a dog. You didn't start looking like you looking and doing like you doing until you started messing around wit him. Brother Bob points his finger toward sister Mae saying; Say what you want Sister Mae; I know what I had to do; said Brother Bob.

Oh yea Brother Bob they brought up in the meeting about you not making the meetings. They said they was going to take the Stewart Board position from you because you stealing the money and not making the meetings. Do you have the $500 dollars donation from the Stewart Board? All the other organizations of the church have turned theirs in accept yours. Sister Mae I keep forgetting it. It's in the house I'll turn it in tomorrow. A voice calls out from the direction of Brother Bob's house: Bob! Bob! The voice walking toward the street where they're standing. Here I am Flo said Brother Bob. Hay you just getting home from the meeting? Asked Sister Flo. Yes it was a long meeting answered Brother Bob. Did you get the donation from the Stewart Board paid? Asked Sister Flo. Yes dear" everything went fine said Brother Bob. Oh hi! there Sister Mae I didn't know that was you. How are you doing? Said Sister Flo. I'm fine replied Sister Mae. You just left the meeting Sister Mae? I have been left the church, I been riding around looking for someone for about an hour and a half. Well I better get back in the house before those kids tear it down. Good to see you Sister Mae. Okay Flo you have a good night. Flo I got somewhere I need to go. I'll see you in a few minutes said Brother Bob. Sister Flo walks on into the house. Hold up! Wait a minute said Sister Mae: You ain't going nowhere. You just stood here and told me you keep forgetting to bring the money to church. But your wife just asked you if you gave the money to the church and if you thanked the Reverend for letting you be late giving it, you also told her yes. I know you ain't been to no meeting because I was there. Man you just stood here and told a couple of great big lies. Why Brother Bob? What are you up to? Brother Bob turns and looks up the street. Do you know what's going through my mind? Sister Mae I don't give a rat's ass what's going through your mind said Brother Bob. You always all up in other people's business trying to start trouble, you need to mine your own business and get a life. Everybody that knows you get the same opinion about you. You are a two faced person. Soon as you get a chance you gonna spread my business all over town. Women stay out of my business and leave me alone. Brother Bob turns and walks up the street. Sister Mae yells and says: Brother Bob this is my business you done stole that church money, I am a member of the church. Brother Bob keeps walking up the street. Sister Mae gets in her car and drives off.

CHAPTER THREE

Reverend Franks was sitting in his living room reclined back in his recliner resting when the telephone rang. Sister Mary called out, "John telephone, its Deacon Smith. He's called one time already this evening." Reverend Franks got up and walked to the phone, "Hello Deacon, how are you this evening?" I'm doing fine Reverend. I'm sorry for bothering you at home, but I been had you on my mind every since the meeting. I hope you don't think I disagreed with what you want to do, because I am with you 100 percent. Going out in the world these days is so dangerous. People are doing so much mischief. What I meant in the meeting was I'm scared you might get robbed or hurt going into those neighborhoods by yourself. "Deacon," Reverend Franks replied. It's good to know you are very concerned about my safety, but we are working for God. Jesus went into all kind of neighborhoods. These people that I'm concerned about are also God's children. " You're right Reverend, I am sorry about my lack of faith," Deacon sighed. Deacon nobody's perfect. Reverend anything you come up with I'm for it okay. Okay Deacon that's good to know. Well Reverend I don't want to take up to much more of your time. I'll let you get back to what you were doing. You have a blessed night said Deacon Smith. Deacon you have one also good night said Reverend Franks.

As Reverend Franks laid the phone on the receiver it rang again. He answered, " Hello!" The voice on the other end replies, "Hello, is this Reverend Franks?" Yes this is. " Hi Reverend, how are you tonight?" this is Sister Mae. " I'm doing fine Sister, and you?" I'm doing fine also Reverend. "What I called you for is to let you know I saw Brother Bob this evening. I went by his house when I left the church. I had to ride around for a while but I found him. He's up to something and it ain't good. He lied to you about him going out of town. He goes down in Tank Town all the time. That's where I saw him going on my way to the meeting this evening. Ain't nothing but trouble down in that hole. He stood on the street in front of his house and lied to Sister Flo about that money he owes to the church and about being at the meeting. She thinks he was at the meeting this evening. He told her he gave you that money at the meeting. He told me not to tell anybody, but Reverend it got away with me so bad I had to tell somebody. That's why I called you," groaned Sister Mae. "Sister, I'm glad you're concerned about him. I had said to myself that I was going to have a private meeting with him. He has missed a lot of meetings," replied Reverend Franks. Reverend when I tried to talk to him, he got mad and told me it wasn't any of my business and that I was always up in people's business. You know I'm not like that. Sister, you have a caring nature for people, but I will talk to Brother Bob okay. Reverend, Brother Bob might be done took that money and brought drugs or something, cause don't nothing good go on down in Tank Town. Okay Sister, I'll talk to him, you calm down and get some rest. " Okay Reverend, thanks for listening to me, goodnight," said Sister Mae. Goodnight Sister, you have a blessed night. Hanging up the telephone, Reverend Franks just sat back in his chair with his hand on his head, shaking his head back and forth.

Sister Mary walked into the room with a smile on her face. "Sister Mae at it again?" asked Mary. " Yes, but I guess she means well," said Reverend Franks. Mary I'm going to the study for a minute and I'm going to ride over to the south side of town for a while okay. Okay John, after I finish the kitchen I think I'm going to lie down. You be careful, she leaned over and gave him a kiss on the lips and told him, "I love you John." I love you to Mary. They looked at each other with big smiles. Mary departed from the room. Reverend Franks went into the study fell to his knees.

Dear heavenly Father, I thank you for your son Jesus, Lord thank you for my life health and strength. Lord, I got your message loud and clear and I am very obedient. Lord, I went to see your children on the south side of town, your children are very lost and confused. Lord, they are ready for your miracle. Lord, guide me to deliver it. Lord I have some members that have gone astray. Lord stay with me as I round them up. Lord, touch all of their hearts, show them the road to take to get to you Lord. Lord, thank you for my wife, continue to bless her with your goodness. Lord I'm going to depart and go check on your children. Stay with me and give me the right things to say. In Jesus name I pray. Amen. Reverend Franks grabbed his keys and headed out the front door.

Brother Bill had made it to the South side of town. He got out of his car and walked down the street. He saw a young man in front of the store cussing and fussing. Brother Bill walked up to the young man and said, " Hey man, how are you tonight." Ben a drunk who lives from day to day focusing on getting a couple dollars to buy him a forty oz beer, and has been through a lot of down falls in life experiencing losing a good job, the woman of his dreams, and his family's trust because of gossip in the streets so he chose to make the streets his family replies, " That man back there owe me some bread and won't pay me. I don't want to have to go to his ass cause it want be pretty. The way I feel his mother, fucking ass would look good cut the fuck up. Ya don't play me like that. Hey man! Who you? The "po po? You got a couple dollars you can let me have to get me a forty? " No, I am not the po po.

The Lord sent me to you to tell you if you follow me I can heal you from wanting that beer. All you have to do is do what I say," said Brother Bill. "You give me a little something on that forty you be done got me man, show you right," said Ben. I can show you a better life. When you think about the life you live, you will wonder how did you live this life style. Brother Bill standing there smiling with a very convincing look on his face. Ben looks up at him shaking his head up and down he points his finger at Brother Bill and says: "Ya know a preacher man named Franks been coming around talking bout God can change our life, he sounds pretty good man. " Yea I know him he's the pastor of my church. He's the one that sent me here to talk to you all because he knows I'm good and for real. Ben speaks up and changes the subject. You gonna give me that what I asked for man? If I give you a couple dollars will you follow me? Yo dog, I'll follow you anywhere! Brother Bill went in his pocket and pulled out some money and said, " Here Ben take this five dollars, I'm going down the street to talk to some of these other people.

"Ben said"; thank You Brother! See ya!" Ben headed toward the store. Brother Bill walked farther down the street to the edge of the store where there was a crowd of young men and women standing around talking loud, some fussing about who owed whom money. Brother Bill enters into the middle of the crowd and yells out, "Hi! How's everybody doing this find evening?" Everybody got silent. Derrick a drug dealer and pimp who runs that side of town and what he says to his people they better jump and do because he is the man speaks up, " Who the hell is you? Looking like you looking, said Derrick. "Ain't nobody told you to come up in here man." Brother Bill standing there smiling speaks up, "My name is Brother Billy Moore. I came out tonight to talk to you all about me helping you'll to change your life styles around for the better. I know I can do it if you all would just follow me." Derrick shaking his head back and forth walking up to him speaks up, "Man you sound like you don' bumped your damn head. We don't know you like that. How in the hell can you change my life around for the better? I make more money than you will ever make. Look around you now. See my girls and this ain't all of them. See man THIS is my turf. Customer's ride, walk or page me for my services. If I can't make it to fill the order then I will send one of my employees. I have people employed all over this town. I have girls to show you a good time and if you want to feel good and mellow at the same time I got anything you want. If you want a job I got that to." Brother Bill still smiling he replies to Derrick, " No thank you brother, I'm not looking for a job. I want to introduce you all to a life that is legal and clean."

Reverend Franks walked up to the edge of the crowd. Anita sees him. She pushes her way through the crowd and stands beside him. All you all have to do is follow me. I have been there don that, and made it by myself. Janice a jezebel who works for Derrick over the girls teaching them how to be good at their tricks in the streets, helping to sell drugs; and you name it, she does it, and who's family disowned her because she didn't add up to their standards, being out on her own at a young age and struggling was introduced to the streets and fast money and the streets that showed her love and became her family walks up to Brother Bill wearing a big smile of seduction on her face. She places her hands upon his chest moving them in circular motion speaks in a very low voice, " You're so cute, I'll follow you, and I know you'll have a better life when I get through with you. Hey by the way everybody calls me Jezebel. Bill, Jezebel can make you feel real good." Brother Bill looks at Janice with a smile on his face, he removes her hands from his chest very slowly and steps back from her. Tina, a seventeen year old young lady with three children and pregnant with the forth one walks up to Brother Bill and speaks up, " Reverend Franks said God can forgive you for your sin if you follow our Lord and Savior Jesus Christ. Brother. Bill is you like him," asked Tina. Young lady I can show you how to turn your wrong doing to good just follow me. Ron a small time Drug Dealer that has murdered several people, works for Derrick and is only 15 years old steps up and speaks in a skeptical tone of voice, " So man you trying to tell us you're like God, the homey you can't see, hear or touch?" So you can work miracles in our lives?" said Ron. Brother Bill is standing there with a half of a smile on his face. The whole crowd was standing there looking at him he spoke up, "You can say that."

Reverend Franks still standing at the back of crowd, Anita still stands beside him. Anita Ward's a cocaine crack addict that wants to be clean so bad. She's the young lady that Reverend Franks saw standing by the paper box. Anita looks up at Reverend Franks and asks, "Reverend, do you know him?" Reverend Franks replied, "Yes he's one of the brothers at my church." "Brother Bill ain't said nothing about God changing his life he talking like he did it himself," said Anita. I know, let me go stop him before he confuses you all anymore. Reverend Franks walked to the middle of the crowd. Everybody started greeting him with smiles, pats on the back and calling out to him, "Hey Reverend Franks!" Reverend Franks through his hands up with a big smile on his face and replied out loud, "Hello everybody! How are you all doing this fine evening?" He walked up to Brother Bill and asked; if he could speak to him in private. They walked a little ways up the street. Reverend Franks stopped and turns to Brother Bill and said, " Brother Bill I have been standing back there listening to you talking to these people. Never one time have I heard you mention God? All I've heard is you telling them is that you can change them if they follow you. The only way these people's lives can change is with the help of the Lord. The little bit of hope and faith in God I have given them you are about to destroy it. You are misleading them. You're supposed to be a messenger of God. What you are being is a false prophet." " Reverend Franks I was about to get around to that. I wouldn't dare mislead them," said Brother Bill. Brother Bill this situation right here is very delicate with these people. We are surrounded with evil demons right now. What you were doing just a while ago was with a negative spirit. I am the only hope these people have. You have to be prayed up to handle these people. They have a little hope now and I am not going to let you take that from them. I have formed a healthy relationship with them. They trust me. So don't be feeding them that false information okay.

Reverend Franks walked back down the street and joined the crowd. Brother Bill stood back and watched them. Ron approached Reverend Franks, " Yo Rev, we missed you at the gym playing basketball with us. " You coming next Saturday," asked Ron? "Yes, I'll try to make it, I had something to do this Saturday. I hate I missed it, because I wanted to put another stump Johnson on you rookies again," replied Reverend Franks. Yea man, you got a dope hook shot. Ron and Reverend Franks gave each other a high five. Brother Bill still observed the relationship Reverend Franks had formed with the young ladies and men of the streets.

Tim, Timothy Miller a very intelligent young sixteen year-old man that trusted his friends and was Janice's nephew, came up to Ron. "Hey Ron! Man what's up?" asked Tim. Yo Tim! What's up wit you man? Both of them gave each other a big hug. Tim replied, on my way home to get ready for work. I saw all of you out here, so I stopped to holler. " Tim man when you off again, I still want to see you high so I can trip," said Ron. Man I told you I don't mess with that stuff. Ain't no future in it any kind of way. "It affects your brain cells," said Tim. "Ahh man, everybody needs to get high at least one time in life. Tim man you know I got your back all of us do. Come by the next time you off," replied Ron. Yo Ron man, a job's open at Wal-Mart. Soon it's going to be two. Come on and put an application in and leave this street life alone. "Man makes an honest living," said Tim. Tim man I got a job; I can't make the money there, that I make here in the streets. Man I make money and have fun doing it, said Ron" Okay man gave you the offer. Change your mind come on by. "Ron, I got to go home to get ready for work. I'm off tomorrow; check you then. Ya know I got to holler at Aunt Janice. Hey love all of ya, bye-bye.

Tim went around the corner of the store to the alley to holler at his Aunt Janice. When he got their Janice, Anita and Reverend Franks was talking. Janice looked up and saw Tim. "Oh Reverend, I want you to meet my handsome nephew Tim. Tim, this is Reverend John Franks," replied Janice. " Hey son," Reverend Franks extended his hand out. Tim shook hands with Reverend Franks. "Good to meet you, how are you this fine evening." asked Reverend Franks. " I'm blessed sir, rushing right now, got to go home and get ready for work," replied Tim. Work! Son how old are you? "Sixteen sir," said Tim. Son, I am really impressed with your positive attitude and spirit you have within you. Where do you work? I work at Wal-Mart on the Blvd. Sir, I have to stay prayed up in order to over power that negative spirit that's after me. My parents told me if I get me a job, they'll help me get a car and they did. They paid cash for it a $1000.00 and gave it to me. I told them I would pay them back in ten months but I'm going to do it in five months at $200.00 a month. All I have is two more payments. My Dad told me when you work for something and trust in the Lord, you'll, be blessed; you know sir, Dad didn't lie. I could be out here slinging drugs and making that fast money, probably would pay for my used car in one lump sum, but out here is of the devil, ain't know future in that stuff. I tell my Aunt and everybody else out here, but you know Rev the Lord knows best. Well I got to go so I can eat and get ready. It was a pleasure talking to you. All you have to do is slip just a little bit, and that devil will win, said Tim. "Son, it was so good to talk to you. You stay in that frame of mind, and stay prayed up, and be blessed, bye son," replied Reverend Franks.

When Tim turns around he sees Ali, a drunk that lost faith in himself, because of family members and friends putting him down all the time, for losing his job and etc. "Yo Ali, Rev this is the best mechanic in the nation, if you can keep him off the juice. All he need is his papers. He can listen to a car engine run, and tell you what's wrong with it. I believe cars talk to him. "Ali I need you to check my car for me again," said Tim. Okay man you know all you got to do is bring it to me, I'll do you right. "Later yall!" said Tim. "Ali man you got it that way with cars?" asked Reverend Franks? Yes sir I love working on cars. "Well son why haven't you went to school to get your license, so you can get a job in one of these big dealerships or garages?" asked Reverend Franks.

I learned how to work on cars by hanging around my uncles' garage when I was a little boy. I would ask him all kind of questions and he took time and patients with me. He would never forget about my questions because when a job come in and it had something to do with a question I had asked, he'd call me and give me a wrench then talk me threw the job. Believe me when he would tell, or show you something, it was right. My Uncle Pill died when I was 18 years old. He was the only one that believed in me. He never downed anybody. Yes, he'd take a drink every now and then, but he didn't drink on the job. He welcomed anybody into his life. He said if he turns somebody away he might be turning Jesus away. When he died a piece of me died with him.

When I graduated from high school, I told my family I wanted to go to school to be a mechanic and work in Uncle Pill's garage. My family downed Uncle Pill, called him an old drunk, talking' about all he had around the garage was drunks and low life people. Throwing in my face that I was going to be just like him but when they need their cars fixed they come find me. I wanted so bad to keep the garage opened but couldn't. I got married, had a beautiful little girl and was buying a home. I got a job working on the docks over town during the day, and would work on cars when I got off that evening, so I could make extra money to open Uncle Pill's garage. I saved enough money to have the lights turned on and to pay two months rent. I took the money to Aunt Duke, she said boy I ain't letting you turn my place to a hangout for low life, no good people. Your own mama doesn't believe in you. Rev. they'd down me so bad I didn't want to go around them, everything I tried to do they had something negative to say about it.

I just started drinking more and more so I could stop thinking about Uncle Pill, and hearing my family down me in my mine. My wife would be fussing about things my family done told her about me. I got tired of feeling sorry for myself. Four years ago I went to work drunk, got on the fork truck and just started driving real careless, almost hitting a co-worker and loading a truck wrong. The driver of the truck reported me. My boss called me to the office; he asked me what have been wrong with me, these last couple of weeks? I told him nothing if he didn't like what I was doing to fire me. He said I was a good worker but he couldn't put up with the attitude I had grown to have. I had been coming in late not pulling my orders; then that. He said he was going to have to let me go. After that I lost my house, wife and car. I just felt like I was a no body. I started hanging in the streets cause these people out here could identify with how I felt.

None of us want to live like this. Our peeps down us so bad. They lie to us until when they want something from us. Like wanting dirty work of some kind done. Reverend Franks you would be surprised who's on drugs of some kind, who's out creeping on their husbands or wives. Po folks can't afford to pay a high dollar hooker or buy powder and crack by the quantities. Man you see a lot out here in the streets. I have been out here for three years. "So Ali, you're George Pills nephew? He uses to fix all our cars, and did real good work. He always had a smile on his face. Everybody loved him. I remember when he died. The church couldn't hold everybody. He touched a lot of lives black and white. He instilled a lot of wisdom and his gift into you. You continue to hold on to that Ali, God can work miracles," said Reverend Franks.

CHAPTER FOUR

On Tim's ride home he was thinking very hard about what Ron had said about everybody gets high at least one time in their life. He thought about if he experienced it he could tell other people how it made him feel. Then he thought about what he didn't know wouldn't hurt him. He got home and sat on the front porch. He thought about it in his mind saying, " It wouldn't hurt me to try it. Ron said he got my back. Then he thought, but I might freak out, I might not be able to handle drugs, and I have never drank a beer. No, I am not going to try it, drugs kill." He got up, went in the house and got ready for work.

Anita saw Reverend Franks. She called out to him, "Reverend Franks!" She ran to meet him. "I called my moms the other day like you told me to do. I told her about the talks you and I have been having. I asked her if she would pick me up so we could talk and told her that I wanted to see ma baby. She told me she wanted so bad to pick me up and bring me home to live, but she was afraid it was another one of my games. I told her it wasn't a game, that I was for real because you had introduced me to a new strength, which was God. She picked me up, and Reverend my mama and baby looked so good to me. I shared with her the scripture Acts 9:18 because I see through a new pair of eyes, like Paul," said Anita.

"Anita, God can fix anything, all you need is a want to and mean it from your heart. All you have to do is believe in him, and have faith," said Reverend Franks. I want my family back so bad. I want them to believe I am for real now. I see what I have done to them, and most of all myself. I have to fix myself, and then I can show them other than telling them. Amen! Anita! that's the attitude to have. Reverend Franks put his arm around her to show that he was very supportive of her. "Reverend can I go to church with you every chance I can?" asked Anita. "Yes child you are very welcome.

"I have been telling a lot of people about how you've helped me to see my wrong doing. They want you to minister to them the way you minister me." " I would be glad to. I tell you what, I will have a program and all of you are very welcome, and then I can minister to everyone. Let me go announce it to them right now." Reverend Franks walks to the middle of the crowd. "Listen up everybody for those of you that don't know me, I am Reverend John Franks, I am the Pastor of Mount Sinai Baptist Church across town at 1631 Elm Street. I'm going to have a program at my church. The name of the program is A New You. I will have to get back with you all tomorrow at this same time with the dates and time. But it will be real soon. And everyone is welcome to come. So make sure to tell your friends. Transportation is no problem. I can arrange for everyone to be picked up if you need it. I will be back tomorrow at this same time, which is 7:00 pm with the dates and time. Will everybody join hands and let me have a word of prayer with you all before my departure."

> *Dear heavenly father; It's me again, Lord thank you so very much for you son Jesus, Lord I want you to touch these people that's in the presence of my voice. Lord you know their needs, wants and don't wants. Lord touch their family's let them know that their love ones out here are tired, they have seen the areas where they are wrong, they want to correct them. They want to come back and be apart of the family again, they have learnt to love them self. Lord you are a heart fixer, you are a mind regulatory, you are the greatest at everything, Lord you said what ever we want ask for it, we know you will be right on time. In Jesus name we pray everybody say A-men.*

Everybody have a blessed night. Reverend Franks and Brother Bill leaves going to their cars.

The crowd is standing around talking among them self. If I start going to church I have to stop getting my drink on. "I'm going to follow Brother Bill he gave me five dollars, and I got me five forties," said Ben. "I ain't going, because my customers will be coming by all day and all night. "I ain't got time for church," said Derrick. I ain't got time either I got it going on, in any way form and fashion, ain't nothing church can do for me," said Janice. "Hey new clients," said Wanda (a prostitute who works for Derrick). "More money," said Shunda another prostitute who works for Derrick. "More and new men," said Dee another one of Derrick's prostitutes. "Yea I'm tired of the same old men day after day. Some new ones would be good for a change," said Gwen (another prostitute working for Derrick).

Listen at all of you, every one of you talking about not going. I have heard you say, you are tired of this life on the streets. The main thing all of us say is we are tired of our family's giving us a hard time. Every one of you have done like me, lied to your family and friends, trying to get them to accept you. But we know the rejection from everybody and everything is because of the life we live. So let's give church a good try, I know I am. I'm going to the alley to study this bible Reverend Franks gave me, anyone want to join me? Anita walks toward the alley.

Reverend Franks and Brother Bill are standing on the street talking. "Reverend, I'm amazed at the affect you have on those people, said Brother Bill. The effect I have on them is being real. I appear to them the way God wants me too. I don't want to give them no kind of false hopes. These people are reaching out for help. What you have been doing is the work of a false prophet, said Reverend Franks. Reverend I still can change them. I can help them, said Brother Bill. Brother, God is the only one that can change them. He can help them only if they want to be helped. Brother Bill, a false prophet is a person pretending and trying to control a message from God. Just think about what I just said okay. Come on let's go home and have a restful night. And I'll see you tomorrow. Reverend Franks and Brother Bill get in their cars, both of them exits in different directions.

On Reverend Franks route leaving the South Side of Town, he sees a car in distress, the closer he get to it the more familiar it looks. When he got upon it, it appears to be one of his elderly member's cars, Mother Moore. Reverend stops get out, he approaches Mother Moore saying, "Mother what's, wrong are you alright?" "Reverend my car just cut off I don't know what's wrong with it. That man over there stopped to help me, but he couldn't pin point the trouble, so he called that other man from the garage on the next street, but I don't think he can find the problem. We had been out here two and a half hours." Reverend Franks walks over to the two men and ask, "Hey what's wrong with it?" The two men raised their heads from under the hood, shaking their heads and replied; "Man I don't know what's wrong with it. The battery is not dead, got plenty fire, alternators strong, belts are in tack, but what's got me puzzled is why it won't say or do anything, when you turn the key. I checked the starter, ignition and everything," said Grady the mechanic. "I guess I'll just call my tow truck." Reverend Franks said, " Grady don't call the tow truck yet, let's try one more thing okay. I'll be right back." Reverend Franks hurried to his car, backed up, and headed in the direction he came from earlier. He stayed gone for about five minutes and returned with Ali. They get out of the car and walked up to the other men.

Reverend Franks introduced Ali to everybody. He told Grady to tell Ali what the car was doing. Grady explained to him that he had no idea what was wrong with the car. Ali asked if he could check the car? Grady told him, "Sure help yourself." Ali grabbed the flashlight. He checked a number of things under the hood. He stepped over to Grady and asked, " Mr. Grady may I use some of your tools?" "Yes son help yourself," said Grady. Ali gathered the tools he needed. He asked Reverend Franks if he would shine the flashlight for him. "Yes son," Reverend replied as he held the light while Ali worked on something at the back of the motor. He rose up and said, "Reverend I think I know what's wrong with it now. Will you hold the light for me inside the car?" "Yes son," said Reverend Franks. Ali looks at Mother Moore, "Mam I'm going to have to take your ignition out, and reconnect the wire and ground. It's going in another direction, because it has shorted out and shut everything down."Mother Moore said, "Okay baby do what you got to do, I just want to get home." Ali continued to work on the car, ten minutes later he was through. He put the key in the ignition, turned it over, and the car started right up.

Reverend Franks walked over to Ali with a big smile on his face. He grabbed Ali's hand shaking it and said, "Boy your uncle taught you good. I knew you could do it. Pill's wisdom is all in you." Grady the mechanic walked over to Ali and shook his hand with a smile on his face and said, "Son what did you do? I checked the fuse box all the fuses was good. "I pulled on the wires that ran into the ignition box a couple of them didn't fill right. I thought about this job Uncle Pill had where this car just shut down. Uncle told me to check out that car, and tell him what I thought was wrong with it. Me and a few other guys, we checked everything we could possibly think of but we couldn't find the problem. Uncle Pill showed us those wires. He said it was amazing what difference some small little wires can make," said Ali. Grady asked, " Son you're Pills nephew?" "Yes sir," replied Ali. " I was really impressed by what I just seen. I been a mechanic for twenty years, thought I knew everything about a car. The only way I would have pin pointed that problem, was with the dependency of modern technology," said Grady. "Grady would you like to have Pills old school skills in your shop?" asked Reverend Franks. "Pill instilled his knowledge in this young man. This young man is just like his uncle, he eats, sleeps and lives to work on cars," said Reverend Franks. " Son where do you work?" asked Grady. "Nowhere sir," replied Ali. "Would you be interested in working for me?" Ali looked up with a surprised look on his face, and then he looked back down, and replied, "Yes sir! But I don't have a mechanic certificate. I never went to school. I wanted so bad to go, but things kept coming up." Ali don't let that stop you, there are schools around here," replied Reverend Franks.

"Grady man don't the Community College have that Vocational of Rehabilitation program still?" "Yes they do have it," replied Grady with a smile on his face. " I wonder if Auto Mechanics is offered in that program?" asked Reverend Franks. "Yes they offer it through the MaGrady Program," said Grady. Reverend Franks walked over with his hand extended and smiling. "So you are MaGrady?" "Yes! I'm give a chance MaGrady. My wife and I started the MaGrady program several years ago, through Vocation of Rehabilitation, purposely to give people another chance to better them self. Both of us have been there, and somebody gave us another chance. The individual will have to qualify to get the assistance then they will do O.J.T. "On the Job Training". Ali, are you willing to do what it takes to qualify?" asked Grady. Ali said, " Yes sir! I'm willing to do anything. Reverend Franks said I'm willing to do anything you all need me to do," replied Ali. Grady shook Ali's hand and said, " Okay son I will start processing papers tomorrow. Here's my card, stay in touch with me. Come to the shop Monday morning at 8:00 a.m." Reverend Franks said, " Ali I'll pick you up Monday morning so you won't have to walk. Grady thank you, and God Bless you. If I don't see you before Monday you have a blessed weekend," said Reverend Franks. Ali shook Grady's hand and said, " Again sir, thank you and sir I want disappoint you. I'll see you Monday early, good night." Ali got in the car and Reverend Franks took him to York Street to drop him off. "Thank you Reverend Franks, and have a good night," said Ali. " Anytime! Ali you have a blessed night," said Reverend Franks still wearing that big smile.

CHAPTER FIVE

Sister Mary was in her living room dusting and straitening up when the phone rang. "Hello! Sister Mary this is Brother Bob, may I speak to the Reverend?" "Hi there Brother Bob, Reverend Frank's not here. I'm expecting him at anytime," replied Mary. "Will you tell him to call me as soon as he get in, I don't care what time it is." " Okay! I'll make sure to tell him bye!" Just as she hung the phone up, Reverend Franks walked through the door. " John! Brother Bob called about two minutes ago, he said for you to make sure to call him as soon as you get in," "Okay thanks, I really need to talk to him anyway," replied Reverend Franks.

Reverend Franks picked the phone up and dialed. 'Hello! Yes may I speak with Bob please?" " This is Bob, is this you Reverend?" " Yes this is," replied Reverend Franks. "Reverend I really need to talk to you as soon as possible. Can I come over right now?" asked Brother Bob. "Yes Brother come on over," said Reverend Franks. "Okay I sure will bye!" replied Brother Bob. Reverend Franks hung the phone up and headed toward the study. "Mary, Brother Bob is on his way over. I need to make a couple of calls. Show him in when he gets here okay." " Okay John, I sure will," replied Mary.

Reverend Franks went into the study and shut the door. He sat down at his desk, fumbled through some papers and finds his calendar. He looked through his roller decks found a number and dialed it, a voice spoke, " Hello!" " May I speak with Sister Dot please?" asked Reverend Franks. " This is Sister Dot." " Sister Dot, this is Reverend Franks." " I know who this is, I know your voice anywhere Reverend, good to here from you. What can I do for you?" Sister Dot replied. " A lot I hope," said Reverend Franks.

"You need me to help you with your books, along with your physical love needs? My husband is out of town, would you like to come over?" asked Sister Dot. " No I wouldn't! I called to ask you to look on the church calendar and let me know the earliest Sunday evening we have opened. I want to have a program. The name of the program will be called **A New You.** I also want you to announce that I will be calling a short meeting with the members immediately after church tomorrow. Have you checked the calendar yet?" " Yes Reverend, we have May 26th, which is one week from tomorrow open," said Sister Dot. " Great! Pencil in the program called A New You (Bury the Devil) at 4:00pm. I want invitations sent to all the churches in the district plus announcements made on the radio stations," said Reverend Franks. "Reverend is this program for those people you have been talking to in the streets?" asked Sister Dot.

"Sister this program is for all of us. The Lord has given me the message to minister to all people, old ones as well as young ones, and this is a powerful message," said Reverend Franks. "Reverend why don't you come over tonight and let me help you with that message. I will make you want to leave Sister Mary," said Sister Dot. "Sister Dot after the meeting tomorrow I need to talk to you okay. Get those announcements out for me. I have to go now. You have a blessed night. Good bye."

Sister Mary knocked and opened the door. She stuck her head in and announced, " John, Brother Bob's here." "Thanks Mary, send him in," replied Reverend Franks. Brother Bob entered the room. He sat in the chair at the front of the desk. "Hey Brother! How are you tonight?" asked Reverend Franks. "Fine Reverend, and you?" replied Brother Bob. "I'm fine, what can I help you with?" "Reverend, I know Sister Mae have been talking to you, and everybody else. She came to see me after the meeting tonight. She asked me why I lied to you about being out of town. I had to tell another lie to cover that lie. I told her that you were lying. Then Flo came out thinking I had been to the meeting, cause I told her that's where I was going, see Reverend that's another lie. That money for the Stewart Board I don't have it. I blew it. I don't have any money to pay it back. I told Flo I paid it tonight. Brother may I ask, what have you been doing, to make you tell all those lies? Reverend this guy I work with, every day he insisted I go with him and his friends to this hole in the wall club in Tank Town. A few months ago I went. I didn't like it the first time. When I went again it was a little better. I told Flo about it, we talked and decided I wouldn't go back anymore. There's gambling, drinking, drugs and all kind of no good woman that hang out there. The guys at work kept teasing me when I would tell them I wasn't going anymore. Saying I was hen pecked. My male ego stepped in to prove to them I wasn't. I went time after time. The more I went the better I liked it. I used my being treasure of the Stewart Board as an excuse to get away from the house. I'd tell Flo I was going to meetings or dinners with you. Just so I could get to Tank Town. Reverend Franks I don't know what to do. It's eating me up. I can't believe I've done this to myself. I don't know why I did it.

"Brother the company you keep you're not aware of but your life style will eventually follow the same path as theirs. You know like the old saying if you're around someone that limps all the time, without you knowing it you'll start limping. Brother you just have to change the company you keep. The ones that are insisting you go astray, their homes and lives are in a bad way already because misery loves company. You can't blame it on no one but yourself. God gives us choices, it's up to us which way to go. If you choose to put your life in jeopardy and loss a lot the choice is yours," said Reverend Franks. "Reverend I just can't tell Flo. I have a good wife and children. I have a family that loves me so much. If I loose them I won't have anything. As many lies I've told Flo, she'll never believe me, or trust me again," said Brother Bob.

Brother Bob as it says in Acts 5:4 "You have not lied to man, you have lied to God," and in Acts 5:30-31, "God raised his son from death, after man had nailed him to the cross to give the people of Israel the opportunity to repent, and have their sins forgiven." So brother you have to ask God to forgive you for your sins and ask him to help you to mend what you have done. Pray about it Brother, God can fix it. God knows if you are for real, ask him to help you to figure out what to do and brother he will give you the answer. Now go home and get a good night sleep. "Okay Reverend, and thanks for listening to me good night." Brother Bob got in his car, routing toward home, his mind still in a state of confusion, he said over and over in his mind, "Lord if I would have just went home to my family instead of going to Tank Town, I wouldn't be in this mess. How can I tell my wife what I'm going through on the inside, and not hurt her and my family?" When Brother Bob turned to head down the street where he lived he saw a car parked in front of his house. He recognized the car instantly. It was his friend from work Jim who's home was torn up, and waned to help brother Bob to tear his home up too.

Brother Bob pulled in his driveway and parked. He immediately got out of the car and rushes over to him. "Hey Bob! I've been looking everywhere for you," said Jim. "Jim man what are you doing at my house? I told you not to be coming here," whispers Brother Bob. "Man I know you wouldn't mine this time. Everybody at Tank Town is asking about you, even Gloria. She told me to find you," replied Jim. "Man quit talking so loud! My wife might here you," said Brother Bob. He looked around to see if Sister Flo was at the window. "Man forget your wife! She'll get over it," said Jim. "Come on man the night is still young. Today is Gloria's birthday, we're celebrating and she wants you to make it complete. Are you coming Bob?" " No! Jim I'm not. Man I have a beautiful woman in the house that loves me very much. I have lovely children that think the world of me. Before I started going down in the hole with you! Man I had a beautiful life. Now my life ain't nothing but a bunch of lies that could tear my world apart. I'm going back to church faithfully. I'm praying to my Lord and Savior Jesus Christ to help me fix what I have done to my family, especially myself. Hey Jim man he can do it. When I was faithfully in the word I didn't have any of this confusion in my life. But now I can't sleep at night, I can't rest during the day, I have to watch what I say, and how I answer questions. I stay very defensive about everything, man I'm tired of that."

"Bob you ain't serious! Are you?" asked Jim. Ain't no fun in all that? Every man needs time for himself, that's what my wife couldn't understand; said Jim. You gonna let your wife dictate to you how to run your life?" asked Jim. Brother Bob answered, " If that's what it takes to get our lives back on track, yes! She can dictate all she wants, because you guys ain't gonna do nothing but keep confusion in my life. You all won't do half of what that sweet woman in that house will do for me. So good night I'm going in the house to my wife."

CHAPTER SIX

The next afternoon Reverend Franks was in the process of opening up the meeting with his members and said, "I want to thank everybody for staying over for this short meeting. Members and friends I'm having a program this Sunday coming May 26th 2005 at 4:00pm. The name of the program is A New You (Bury the Devil) with a powerful message. The Lord has laid it heavy on my heart to minister to everyone. I'm sending out invitations through the mail, TV, radio, on the Community Calendars and word of mouth. I want all of you to extend the invitation to everyone you see. This ministry will start briefly in our bible study, which will be based on worldly living because a lot of people are not aware of their worldly lives. All of you that can need to come out to bible study and bring someone with you. If there is no other business that we need to discuss let's stand and be dismissed."

Sister Mae raises her hand. "Yes Sister!" "Reverend we would like to know the status on that donation money from the Stewart board that Brother Bob was suppose to submit." "Sister the report on all the organizations will be read in the church business meeting. I don't have the date of the meeting at hand now. It should be posted in the church bulletin of your program today." "Well Reverend, you know he don't have the money because he lied to me, and on you also. I want to know what he did with our money, probably blown it in Tank Town," said Sister Mae. "Sister everything has been taken care of okay, you don't have anything to worry about," said Reverend Franks. "Oh! You done talked to him? Good! He ain't nothing but a liar! Talking about I be in every bodies business said," Sister Mae. Sister Lily spoke up," Well Mae he didn't lie cause you do stay up in people business all the time." "Reverend is the meeting over?" asked Sister Mae as she stood up. "Cause I ain't got to stay here and let people talk about me like this." "Everybody stand and join me in a word of prayer, let's bow our heads," replied Reverend Franks as he prays.

Dear heavenly Father we come before you with our heads bowed and hands joined, some hearts are burdened and some confused. Lord you already know everybody's heart, you know every bodies mind, you know what they are thinking right now. Lord bless us in every way you see fit. Lord this program you have laid on my heart, give me the strength, knowledge and wisdom to get your message out. Lord touch everybody that's in the sound of my voice, Lord touch their family's, bless them the way you see fit. Lord touch those lost souls turn them around, head them on your straight and narrow, Lord help me to find the right words, the right message to lead them to you. Lord I am obedient to you, I love you and your son Jesus, this is my prayer Amen. We are now dismissed. "Everybody try to make it to bible study Wednesday evening," announced Reverend Franks.

Everybody left except Brother Bob and Sister Flo. "Reverend Franks you got a minute?" asked Brother Bob. "Yes brother, what can I help you with?" "Reverend, I told Flo I wanted me and her to meet with you as soon as possible, so I could share with her what I shared with you last night. Do you have just a few minute?" said Brother Bob. "Sure take as much time you need, let's have a seat," replied Reverend Franks. Reverend Franks and Flo sat down; Brother Bob remained standing and turned to Flo. "Flo I shared with Reverend Franks the wrong doing I've been doing for the last couple of months. I have been lying to you about going to church meetings. I lied about the $500.00 for the Stewart board. I blew the money hanging in Tank Town with the guys I work with. I have done things that I am scared to share with you because I don't want to lose you and the kids. Baby I am so sorry and I will do anything to make it up to you, will you forgive me?" Flo sat there for a few seconds and just looked at Bob. She replied, "Bob, yes I'll forgive you, because I'm one of God's children and you're my husband. I love you. Bob we took those vows eleven years ago for better or worse. Being married to you all these years I know you about as good as you know yourself. I know your daily patterns. I know about what you will say, about what you think when you're not feeling good just by how you look and act. I can tell you if it's your head, leg or toe that aches. So don't you know that I detected that evil spirit that came home in my Bob late that Friday night, because my sweet Bob left home that morning, but that evil spirit came home in him late that night? I know you were seeing other women, using drugs and God knows what else because the distance you showed me. We never communicate the way we use to. Your mind was always occupied with something else and all I could do was pray and give you to the Lord." "Flo can things be the way they use to?" asked Bob. "Bob I don't know! If it's God's will," replied Flo in a very uncertain voice. She stood and started to walk away. She stopped, turn around, took a few steps back towards Brother Bob and said, " Bob you hurt me and the kids. Time can heal the hurt but you have to earn the trust back." Bob took Flo's hand and asked, " Flo, what do I have to do?" Flo looked at him and replied, "Do you have to ask? The meeting is over for me because I don't want to know no more of what you did out in that world. I gave you to God, he has handled it this far and I'm going to leave you with him. I got to go check on our children before they tear something down to the ground. Thank you, Reverend Franks for listening. Oh yea! Bob I paid the church the $500.00 for you. The Reverend and I have already had this conversation about you. Take all the time you need. I'm going out here with the children. Sister Flo left out.

Brother Bob turned to Reverend Franks. "So Reverend you been aware of my wrong doing?" asked Brother Bob. "Yes, Sister Flo came to Mary and I a couple of months ago. She was very hurt and concerned." "Reverend, why didn't she say anything to me?" "Would it have made a difference if she'd said something about what you were doing? Remember you were suppose to have been working, or at a church meeting. Brother your ways and actions spoke a lot louder than words. You didn't fool anybody but yourself. I don't live with you and I saw the change in you very much. Just like your wife told you she gave you to God, she knew she couldn't handle it and that it was too tough for her. Now it's left up to you. Let's go home and eat some dinner with our families. I have another appointment to make.

Reverend Franks goes home, sat down and ate dinner with Mary. He told her the plans about the program next Sunday. His main focus was keeping the street people encouraged about attending. Mary spoke up, " John you have planted the seed and it's growing beautifully. You have those people's trust, it's not you that's doing it, its God using you. Just continue to do what you're doing." John walked over to Mary and gave her a big hug and kiss and said, " Mary I love you very much, and you are so good for me." "I love you to John," Mary replied in a soft voice. "I got to go announce the meeting to Anita and the rest." "Okay John, be careful."

John drove to the corner store, parked the car and walked through the path beside the store. The first person he saw was Anita. He called out to her, " You're just who I'm looking for. I know I'm a little early, but I was on my way to pick up a couple of things on this side of town. I came by to see if I saw you all. The program I told you all about is going to be this coming Sunday at 4:00pm. Here are some flyers, past them out to some people for me. I'm going to put some in this store, and on some of the poles." "Oh yea! How are things with you?" asked Reverend Franks.

"Things are great. I'm sorry I didn't go to church with you today, I took the bus to my mothers this morning. She had a big dinner. My grandmother and some of my cousins were there. I enjoyed being around my mama and baby but with the rest of them I felt so out of place and a funny feeling came over me, like I didn't belong there. They all treated me nice like they were glad to see me. My cousin Cindy, she smoke blunts, she asked me if I still blazed? I told her hell no! I have been clean for two weeks. She said, "Girl you'll go back to the pipe, ain't nothing wrong with doing a little something, something every now and then." Reverend Franks cautiously replied, " Anita that comment your cousin made wasn't nothing but the devil speaking through her, trying to get you to get back on the drug. You be strong and rebuke that devil in the name of the father, the son and the Holy Spirit. Tell Satan to get behind you." Anita speaking with a confused tone in her voice, "Reverend after she said that, I really felt so bad. I just wanted to leave and find some crack. I wanted to just get so high so I could lose the feeling that was going on inside of me. I told my mama I was leaving because I had something to do. She pulled me to the side and asked if everything was all right. I told her, "Yes mama, I got Jesus deep inside of me," and then I kissed her and my baby.

I grabbed my bible out of my bag and held it tight in my hand. I was walking and praying. It's so hard! Reverend I prayed that taste for crack out of my mouth. "Amen! Anita I'm so proud of you," replied Reverend Franks. That is a testimony and a half. Have you seen the rest of your friends that was here last night? "Yes they're in the alley on the street over. Come on we can go through the path. I need to go to the store right down the street for a minute. Then I'll take you to them, through the path. They'll still be there, they ain't going nowhere for a while. All of them have congregated in the alley that they fixed up for their convenience.

CHAPTER SEVEN

The alley's decor consists of an old double lawn chair, some worn kitchen chairs, a table, two old mattresses, two beat up trash cans and two five gallon plastic paint buckets, which they used for end tables. The background was the view of two old stripped down rusty cars sitting on blocks. Around them were empty wine and beer bottles, beer cans and etc. Sitting on the kitchen table was a big boom box with some loud Ron DMC on blast. Ron, Ben and Ali were sharing some new dance moves that they call themselves inventing.

Ron looks up, " Yo Tim! What's up? Saw you pass yesterday, musta been going to Wal-Mart to do the job thang." " Yea man! Some of us do make a living honesty. I asked for some over time, cause I'm trying to pay my car off. I just got two more payments and it will be mind," Tim said with a smile. Ron spoke up with a boasting tone of voice, "Man if you work for Derrick in just a few days you can pay that car off and still have money in your pocket." Ron pulled a roll of money out of his pocket, it depends on how much work you put in. Tim walked closer to Ron with a serious tone in his voice, " Man I ain't got time for that dirty money. There's no future in selling or using drugs. Ron man Wal-Mart has a job opening that came open yesterday. I've already talked to my boss about you. Ron man come on, get a life you'll appreciate it better. You want have to continue to look over your shoulders." "Tim man, I know what you're saying, but Wal-Mart could never put the paper in my pocket like this." Ron pulled back out his roll of money laughing," And this is just today."

Tim turns and look around at everybody, " You know all of you out here are older than I am except Ron and Robbie. Robbie is only 13 years old and is a little boy that is mislead by Derrick, the drug dealing, pimp. Robbie thinks Derrick is the man because he has a lot of money, a bad car, a bad crib and he bling-blings. I can see the harm you all are doing to your lives. The money, drugs, the tricks and even my Aunt Janice, but I still love all of you. I love being around you all. Ya'll good people even though I still don't like what you do." Everybody laughed.

Tim gave Janice a big hug and patted her on the back. "Tim man you off today ain't you?" asked Ron. "Yea and glad of it to. I came to hang out with ya'll for a while," said Tim. "Tim you gonna try a little something, something so we can see you high?" asked Ron. "Man no! I ain't ever wanted to," said Tim. Tim started thinking to himself. "Should I try some? A little bit shouldn't hurt me; I've never tasted beer. I wonder what does it feel like to be high or drunk. Everybody needs to experience stuff every now and then." Ron interrupted Tim's thoughts. "Tim man you off today come on and try a little something. I bet you're a trip high. Come on man so we can bug!" said Ben. Everybody chimed in saying, " Yea man! Come on." "Come on Tim man, trust me it want hurt you, I got your back," said Ron. "Okay I'll try a little bit man, but I won't make it a habit," said Tim.

"Yo Ron! We out of brew," yelled Ali. "Okay we can go over the way and buy some more. Here Tim hold my piece for me. Old boy got that metal detector at both back and front door. Come on Ali let's go and hurry back, I can't wait to see ma man high. This going to be a trip and a half," said Ron. Ron and Ali took off for the store. Tim stuck the gun down in his pants. The rest of them were laughing and talking about Tim getting high for the first time.

Ron and Ali returned with a case of beer, a bottle of liquor and some wine. "Tim we're back here man, here's your first brew and take this pill, you can wash it down with your brew," said Ron. "What kind of pill is this?" asked Tim. "Just some mild acid, it won't hurt you, it'll just make you feel mellow," replied Ron. Tim put the pill in his mouth and washed it down with beer. Ron fired up a joint laced with crack. "Here Tim take a puff of this man this will make you feel real good," said Ron. Everybody continued to laugh while watching Tim. Tim just stood there looking around at everybody. Tim grabs Ron by the arm, " Ron man I feel funny, I don't like this feeling. Man who is that?" asked Tim pointing at a man that had just walked up. "Oh that's one of Derrick's customers." "Derrick man there's Gee!" yelled Ron. Derrick and Gee went around the bushes. Tim was just standing there looking around at everybody. They started calling his name. He was looking around like he was scared to death. Ron started calling him and at the same time walked up to him. "Tim! Tim!" Ron called. "Man what's up?" he asked. Tim started backing up. "Tim man what's wrong?" asked Ron.

Tim started reaching for Ron's gun he had stuck down in his pants. Ron saw him reaching for the gun. Ron talking to Tim in a begging tone, " Tim man no! Handle it man, everything's going to be all right, handle it man, it's me man Ron! No! Tim! No!" "Git away from me! Git away from me!" yelled Tim. "Tim man it's me Ron! I ain't gonna bother you." Tim pulls the gun out and points it at Ron and then around at everybody else. Everybody starts running trying to find somewhere to hide. Janice rushed over to Ron. She pats Ron on the shoulder speaking softly, " Tim baby this is Aunt Janice, everything's going to be alright, please put the gun down please! You got to let the high wear off of ya. Please Tim put the gun down." Tim continues backing up and pointing the gun, looking like he had to protect his life, like there wasn't anything or anybody familiar to him at all. He act like he was in a enemy camp, saying to himself if anyone move I'll shoot you. "Git away form me! Git away from me! I'll kill you!" he yelled.

Tim starts shooting. Janice and Ron hollers, " NO! No! No!" Everybody run and hid. Derrick run from behind the bushes with his gun in his hand. Once Derrick was in Tim's sight, Tim opened fire on him. Derrick fired one shot and hits Tim in the chest. Tim fell to the ground. Everybody peeped out to see if they could come out of hiding. Kevin a cocaine crack addict on the down low was lying on the ground holding his shoulder, a bullet had hit him. Tim was lying on the ground, "dead" shot through the chest.

Janice ran over to him calling, " Tim! Tim! Baby git up! Lord please don't let him be dead!" Ron walks very slowly over to him and fell to his knees. Reverend Franks and Anita run fast as they could; both of them saying, "What happened? What happened?" Everybody was scared to death. "What in the world happened here?" Reverend Franks asked checking for a pulse, and then a heart beat. He took his jacket off and covered Tim up. "Somebody call 911 and hurry," yells Reverend Franks. Anita kneeled down and asked, "Ron what happened?" Ben hollers, "Oh shit! Kevin's been shot!"

Sirens started coming from everywhere. Two police officers rushes on the scene and immediately check Tim. They stood up shaking their heads, "He's dead," said one of the policemen. He calls in on his radio, "Gun shot victim, dead on the scene." They covered him up with a sheet. "Officer, this young man has been shot in the shoulder," said Reverend Franks. The policeman called over the radio, " Need an ambulance for a victim, shot in shoulder on same scene." The policeman looks around and hollers out, " I need a statement on what went on here from some of you." He walks over to Reverend Franks. "Sir can you fill me in on what happened here?"

"Officer, I don't know that's what I'm trying to find out. I'm Reverend John Franks and this is Anita Ward. We were coming through the path over there. We heard an outburst of hollering then continuous shots going off. When we got here this is what we found," said Reverend Franks. The ambulance got there and checks Kevin putting him on a stretcher to take him to the hospital. They unloaded another one to take Tim. Anita still kneeled down beside Ron with her arm around him. She helps him to his feet after the EMT's took Tim away. The girls helps Janice up and sat her down. "Ron come over here," said Anita.

"Man what happened? You got to tell us what happened to Tim. The Police got to know. The police and Reverend Franks are standing there listening. Ron looks up at Anita, tears streaming down his face. "Anita ma boy's gone, he's really gone, and it's like I killed him. I done smoked people before, but I ain't ever felt like this." "Ron, Tim was your best friend, you're feeling hurt in your heart," said Anita. "Anita I didn't know it would do him like that. I thought it would give us a good laugh to see him high. I gave him the drugs; I insisted "on and on" that if he tried it for the first time, it wouldn't hurt him. Anita he just freaked out all of a sudden." "Ron who did the shooting?" asked Anita." Earlier I had given Tim my piece to hold for me; while me and Ali went to the store to get some beer. Anita I could trust Tim with my life". I had forgotten he had my piece. When he freaked out, he pulled my piece and points it at all of us like he didn't know who we were. I was "calling him and "telling him it's me man Ron! But he just open fire and acted like he was scared to death; like we were going to hurt him. He just couldn't handle the drugs. Tim was deep. He always preached to us about drugs was wrong, using and selling. His motto was, "Say no to drugs." I guess we put to much pressure on him about trying some. He stayed on me to get a job with him at Wal-Mart and make a honest living. If he hadn't taken that pill and hit that laced joint, he'd be here now. He wouldn't hurt a flea," said Ron staring into space.

"Ron how did Tim get shot?" asked the Policeman. Ron looked at Anita, looked at the policeman very slowly, and he hung his head then replied, "Derrick had walked off with some of his friends when Tim started shooting. Derrick ran to see what was going on. Time Derrick got in sight Tim started firing at him. Derrick shot him before he knew who he was. Tim was out of control. That's Tim's Aunt over their Janice, she'll tell you he was out of control."

Janice was still crying wishing this part of her life was a nightmare and wishing she'd wake up. The girls were standing by Janice's side, trying to console her knowing her heart that was filled with grief. The Policeman and Reverend Franks walked over to her. "Janice I'm so sorry about what just happened to Tim," said Reverend Franks. "Reverend, Tim was all I had, he was the only one in my family that would come to see about me. He never touched any kind of drugs or alcohol. I should've stopped him before he took that pill and hit that joint. His body wasn't use to it and he didn't know how to handle it. My family's going to blame me. They blame me for everything bad that happen." "Janice, I need to get a statement from you," said the policeman. "Girls will you excuse us?" asked Reverend Franks. The girls walked over to where Anita and Ron were sitting.

"Janice in your own words, tell us what happened." said the policeman.

"Well officer all of us was right here laughing, talking, having fun, drinking and getting high as usual. Tim came by. Everybody always dissing him and calling him a six toe because he didn't drink or use drugs. He always got on all of us about what we did but today Ron, Ali and some of the other guys offered the drugs and something to drink to him and he gave in. It shocked me when he said, "Okay he'd try some just this one time," so he did it. Ron had given him his gun to hold for him while he went to the store, I guess Ron forgot about getting his gun from him because everybody was excited and wanted to trip on seeing Tim high for the first time. I guess when those drugs and alcohol kicked in, it ran Tim crazy poor thing couldn't handle it. He grabbed the pistol from his pants where he had it tucked and just started shooting at anything that moved. Derrick had walked up the way, when he heard the shots he ran back. When Tim saw him he opened fire dead at him. Derrick acted instantly and shot back hitting him in his little chest. I can't believe he's gone. He's so young, he just turned 16 three months ago." "Thank you Janice, by the way what's your last name?" "Miller! Replied Janice, officer the same as Tim's. His name is Timothy Miller," replied Janice.

"I need all of you to stay in town. Don't go anywhere until we've done some more investigating on this case," said the officer. "Okay officer everybody understands," said Reverend Franks. "Officer, please take my name and number, if you need to talk to them again, I'll bring them down town," said Reverend Franks. "I need to talk to Derrick, where is he?" "Yes where is Derrick?" asked Anita. "He's sitting on the ground behind that tree," said Ben pointing at the tree. The policeman and Reverend Franks walked over to him.

"Are you Derrick?" asked the policeman. Derrick shook his head yes. "Did you shoot Timothy Miller?" asked the officer. Derrick shook his head yes. "An investigator will be out to talk with you very soon. Do you have a problem with that?" He shook his head no. "He'll be here officer, thank you for everything," replied Reverend Franks. The policeman left. Reverend Franks stayed behind. He walked around checking things out. He saw a little boy hiding behind the trashcan crying. "Son is you alright? Who are you?" asked Reverend Franks reaching his hand out to him and helping him to stand up. Looking around at everybody he asked, "Who's child is this, and what's he doing hanging in a place like this? Son how old are you?" asked Reverend Franks.

"My name is Robbie and I'm 13 years old." Anita walked over to Reverend Franks, she whispers; he's a friend of Derricks, I think he's going to teach him how to push drugs. Lord help these people. That boy's nothing but a baby. Robbie where's your mother and father? Asked Reverend Franks. "They at home getting high on some crack. They don't know I'm gone," said Robbie.

" Robbie if your grandmother knew you were anywhere near here she'd cut your tail good," said Anita.

"Anita! Just like Derrick said, just because you hating you want to cut a brother out of some quick paper," said Robbie. "I want you to live a long good life. I don't want what happened to Tim to happen to you. Tim's life was cut very short," said Anita. "Ya, see Derrick is the man. He got Tim before Tim got him or us, because we his peeps. I want to be just like Derrick, he got all kinda money, cars, a phat crib and women," replied Robbie. Derrick stood there listening to Robbie with his head down. "Robbie so you think Derrick shot Tim because he was protecting what was his?" asked Reverend Franks. "Yes, Derrick takes care of his peeps. He'll cap anybody that mess with us." Derrick comes up behind Robbie. " Robbie!" Robbie turned around and looked up at Derrick. He saw the tears rolling down Derrick's face.

"Derrick what's wrong?" ask Robbie, "Somebody messing wit you again? Hey man! You know I got yo back," said Robbie. "No man, nobody's messing with me. Derrick put his hands on Robbie's shoulders and looked him in the face. "What's messing with me is listening to you talk and Tim's death. Little man I have been misleading you. I didn't realize it until now. What the Reverend and Anita are trying to tell you is the life I live is a very dangerous life style. I can be living today and dead tomorrow. You want me to tell you what keep going through my mine?" Robbie shook his head yes with a confused look on his face. "Robbie the main reason I shot Tim is because I was scared that those bullets were for me." Derrick kneeled down to one knee and pulled Robbie to him looking him in his eyes. "Little man, please try and understand what we are trying to say. Okay! Man I sale drugs, I sale drugs to anybody that want it so I can make fast money. I thought those bullets were coming from an angry husband because of me selling his wife drugs, or pimping his wife to some other man. It could have been a parent mad because I sold drugs to their child or pimped their daughter or even someone I've talked a lot of shit to or cussed out. Robbie if it hadn't been for me Tim would still be alive right now. The drugs he used to freak him out, were my drugs." Tears streamed down Derricks face. "Ron was selling them drugs for me. Everybody here right now could be dead cause there was a lot of bullets flying. Tim was a good innocent young man; we influenced him to do something he didn't want to do. He trusted us, his friends. We lead him to believe he would be all right. He tried it and it caused him his life. What a price to pay. Friends don't influence you to do something to hurt yourself, they tell you things to keep you safe from harm so man you go to your grandmother's okay. I would take you little man but I got to wait on the investigator. Think about what I said okay! Love ya." "Derrick I'll take him

by his grandmothers," said Reverend Franks. "Anita, will you ride with us?"
"Oh ya! Sure Rev," replied Anita.

"Everybody I'm so sorry for what happened here today," said Reverend
Franks. "Janice, Mrs. Franks and I are so sorry. Our hearts go out to you and
the family. If there's anything I can do for you and the family please call us.
My reason for coming here today was to tell you the date and time of the
program called, "A New You." The program will be 4:00pm Sunday. I'm also
having bible study Wednesday night. I would like for all of you to attend.
Reverend Franks, Robbie and Anita leaves. Derrick runs after them calling,
"Reverend Franks!" Reverend Franks stopped and waited on him. "Reverend
Franks I want to thank you for being here for us. We will be at your program
just for you. I feel so bad about Tim. Why did it have to happen to him?"
"Derrick, God sends us messages, sometimes an innocent person suffers just
like God's son Jesus suffered and died for us. God never make mistakes. Tim's
death was in God's plan and it has a powerful message behind it for all of us.
Tim's work here on earth is over. God has plans for him up there with him.
Derrick here is my phone number if you need to talk or anything no matter
what time call me. Oh yea! Come to the program for yourself. It won't do you
any good if you come just for me," said Reverend Franks. "Thanks Rev.," said
Derrick. Derrick ran back to the alley.

Reverend Franks headed to the car, Anita and Robbie stood by the car
waiting on him. "Come on Robbie let's get you to your grandma," said
Reverend Franks. They crawled in the car, Anita sat in the front on the
passenger side of Reverend Franks and Robbie sat in the back seat. "Reverend
you go up the street and take the first right, up two more blocks take a left on
Cob's, she lives in the fourth house on the right. Robbie's mama and daddy
live right there on the left," said Anita. Reverend Franks followed Anita's
directions and went straight to Robbie's grandmother's house. Reverend
Franks pulled in front of the house. He and Anita walked Robbie to the
porch and rang the doorbell. Robbie's grandma answers the door. Reverend
Franks politely says, " Hello mam my name is Reverend John Franks pastor
of Mount Sinai Baptist Church located across town, this is Anita Ward. This
is your grandson Robbie? Yes he is answered Robbie's grandmother. He was
in the alley just a couple streets over replied Reverend Franks. A shooting
took place a few hours ago unfortunately a 16 year old got shot and killed. I
found your grandson hiding behind one of the trash cans."

"Excuse me Reverend, you all please come in. Have a seat by the way my
name is Edna Manning, my husbands at work he should be home in the next
half hour. Thank you all so much for bringing Robbie here. I've told Robbie
so many times about hanging out in those drug-infested streets. His mama,
my daughter she has a bad problem with drugs. She and her husband both

use. You see Reverend when Robbie was five years old his mama Niece got with the wrong crowd. They introduced her to drugs. Niece and Robbie's daddy Pete separated. Pete took Robbie from Niece. He called me and asked me if I would help him with Robbie. That was the happiest day of my life because I thought I would never see my grandson again. Niece caused all kind of confusion for Pete about Robbie but she didn't want that baby so Pete took him and left town. He couldn't find any body he could trust to keep Robbie so he called me and asked if I'd help with him if he moved back to town. I told him yes I'd be glad to. Pete moved back and got a job driving trucks long distance. Niece heard in the streets Pete had moved back. She came by my house, that's when she found out I was keeping Robbie for Pete. She questioned me about why Pete wouldn't let her know he was back in town because she missed her son. I told her because of her habit and the company she kept. That's why he took the boy from her before. She promised if he let her back in the boy's life, she would straighten up. She started hanging around more often, spending time with Robbie, so Pete gave in for Robbie to spend some nights with her. She stayed sober for about a year, and then things started going down hill again.

Somebody called DSS on her because she was leaving Robbie by himself or having him out in the streets all times of night. She liared her way out of that. I would talk to her and she'd just lie to me. She went to rehab and got clean again. This time it lasted about a year and a half maybe two years. She met Joe and married him, that's who she's with now. He turned her out again. Joe's nothing but a crack head. All they do is get high, fuss and fight. That's how Robbie met Derrick. He thinks Derrick's the coolest man on earth. I told him Derrick wasn't good for him. That's why he likes to stay with his mother so he can run wild. If I ask her anything about that boy she'd lie and say everything was all right and that he stayed at home or he was hanging out with the little boys down the street that's his age. She does that to keep the heat off of her, because she never knows where that boy is. Pete told me last week that he's talked to a lawyer about him and I getting legal custody of Robbie. Until then I can't stop her from taking the boy from my home." "Ms. Manning, I'm so sorry that you're going through this confusion, but you keep the faith. If there's anything I can do just give me a call. I have put together a program at my church Sunday coming at 4:00pm called, " A New You." It's a message from God to minister to people that's going through lives down falls in every category. You and your family's invited and oh yea try to get your daughter and her husband to come. Robbie you listen to your grandmother, grandfather and daddy okay they love you very much. Do you remember what Derrick told you about his mistake?" Robbie shook his head yes, sitting there with his head down.

Reverend Franks stood and walked over to Ms. Manning, extended his hand out to shake saying, "Ms. Manning again it was so good to meet you. Anita and I have to go. I will keep you and your family in my prayers. If there's anything we can do please call me here's my card." Reverend Franks headed for the door, Anita followed behind him.

He dropped Anita off at the corner store. She thanked him for everything and assured him that she would see him at church. Anita went into the store to buy her soda and exited the store taking the path to the alley. Someone called out, " Anita!" Anita turned around. There stood Randy, her little girl's daddy. He walked up to her, "Hey baby! Been looking for you," giving her a hug. Anita pulled away from him. "Randy what are you doing here? I thought you left town for good?" replied Anita. " I did baby. I missed you. You not glad to see me?" said Randy. "It's not like that, I'm going through some thangs now. Got a lot of stuff on my mine." "Like what," asked Randy?

"You know Tim got accidentally shot and killed today. It's rough on all of us." "Yea I heard about that. Everything's going to be all right, I'm here now. How's my baby girl doing?" asked Randy "She's fine, me and mama's working things out finally. She gave me a hundred dollar gift certificate to buy me some cloths at Wal-Mart. She's beginning to believe in me, and I'm going to prove to her that I've changed my life for the better. Randy, I've given my life to God. He has done great things in my life in just a short length of time. He has brought my mama, daddy and my baby back into my life. I'd forgotten who the real Anita really was. You know Anita's a good loving person that wants to be somebody." "Come on girl, you bull shiting. Let's go over to my dog's house and celebrate me being home." "No Randy! I don't go around those people no more cause I'm no more one of them. All they'll do is entice me to use. I will always be an cocaine, crack addict but today I'm sober, clean, and drug free. "Damn Anita, look where you're headed to the alley where the kingpin of the drugs live, Derrick!" shouted Randy.

"Derrick knows where I'm coming from. He and all of them know I have changed my life for the better. Tim's death woke them up. It was Derrick's drugs that made Tim freak out. If they hadn't enticed Tim to use he'd be here now. Get out of my way Randy I got to check on them in the alley," shouted Anita. "Check on them in the alley for what?" asked Randy. "To see how they are doing. They feel bad about Tim's death. Tim was a God sent young man. He helped me out. We talked a lot about the bible. We shared a lot of our thoughts. Some of the things he shared with me worked. He was young but wise," explained Anita. "What ya gonna do when you leave the alley?" asked Randy. "I told my mama I had a surprise for her and that I would call her about 3:00pm and tell her. I've been baby- sitting and saving my money. I'm gonna take mama and my baby out to eat." "Anita let me go with you all."

"No Randy, you the reason I got on drugs and my life went bad. You should change your life around also. Randy why don't you try God? You would like it. I got to go, you have a blessed day." Anita headed to the alley.

Randy walked to the front of the store. He stood there like he just lost his best friend. He walked over to the pay phone, picked up the receiver and dialed a number. "Hello is this Ms. Ward?" he asked. The voice on the phone replied, " Yes this is Ms. Ward." "Ms. Ward this is Randy, Mira's daddy, how're you doing?" "I've been doing fine," said Ms. Ward. "Well, that's good, how has Mira been doing?" "She's doing fine," said Ms. Ward. "That's great Ms. Ward. Anita told me to call you. You know she told you she had a surprise for you. Her surprise is that she and I have been keeping in touch with each other since I been gone. I got back yesterday morning and we been together every since I got here. We decided to get married and have a happy home her, Mira and me. We are just about off of drugs; with the help of God we will make it. Okay Ms. Ward we will talk about it at dinner, see you then," said Randy.

Anita arrived in the alley Derrick yelled, " Anita! What's up? Anita! Have you seen Randy? That stupid nigger been here "bugging". We told him how you ain't the same person he knew, that you've turned your life around clean and free," said Derrick. "Yeah, I saw him just a while ago," Anita replied. "Never mind him, how are all of you making it?" she asked. "We doing good as good can be," replied Derrick "I got to make it to Wal-Mart and buy me something new then call my mama and tell her to meet me down town so I can take her and my little girl out to eat." Ron walked up. "Anita you better call her before that crazy ass Randy do. He was tripping a few minutes ago, he said he was gonna call your mama and fuck your world up show nuff. I told him if he did, I'd fuck his world up," Ron said. Anita with a worried look on her face paced back and forth, "Lord Yall I hope he ain't called her, thang's going to good with us. I got to go call her, anybody got a quarter?" "Here Anita use my cell phone," said Derrick reaching it to her.

Anita dialed the number. "Hello mama, this is Anita, how you and Mira doing? Mama what's wrong? Did Randy call you? But mama he's lying, I just seen Randy a few minutes ago and told him he was no longer a part of my life. No mama, I'm not lying, mama please believe me. No! Mama; don't say that, I didn't tell him to call you. Yes I still got the gift certificate; I been working and still got all my money. Can I still come over to see yall? Mama, Randy's nothing but the devil, don't let him kill what we've built. Mama no! Don't hang up." Anita fell to her knees crying. Derrick helped her to her feet, put his arms around her and held her saying, "Anita baby, Randy was wrong for doing that, that's nothing but the work of the devil." "Derrick he told my mama I was still using, I been clean a month now I got money in my pocket right now. I don't want drugs I want my family. I want them to trust me. Now they think I'm just a big liar as usual. All this hard work I did down the drain. They'll never believe me again," she cried. Anita's heart felt heavy, mind broken, focusing on dreams she had for the near future and of the return of her new found life and family. "Derrick I feel so numb, confused and betrayed. My mama was just waiting for me to mess up. She never had faith in me." "Anita don't say that. She probably feels the same way you do right now. She's probably running things through her mind also. Anita don't give up now okay." "But Derrick what am I going to do? I had a lot to do with Tim's death. I told Tim it was all right to try a little bit of drugs, that God will forgive him for it, but God didn't forgive him, he took his life. Now God took my mama and baby from me. Randy's right! I ain't been doing nothing but bull shiting, this ain't the life for me. I got the reputation as a drug addict, I might as well be one to the fullest." "No Anita! Don't talk like that," said Derrick, come on let's go back to the alley. "No Derrick not right now, you go on I'll be just fine. Here comes Randy he'll give me a hit cause you won't." "No Anita! Come go with me, don't hook back up wit him," pleaded Derrick. Derrick tried to pull her by the arm, Anita pulled away from him. She shouted, "Derrick leave me the fuck alone, I know what I'm doing!" "Okay! go on then, and fuck up! It's your life," Derrick shouted back.

Derrick stood and watched her walk up to Randy. She hugged him and told him, "Randy baby I need a hit bad." "That's my Anita," said Randy. He put his arm around her, his other hand in his pocket, and pulled out a blunt and handed it to her. He told her, " Come on let's go down to my boy's house for the other stuff." They walked on down the street together. Derrick stood looking at them walk away, knowing how hard Anita worked to stay clean and sober. The struggle she went through to win her mothers faith. In just a split second she made a complete turn around.

CHAPTER EIGHT

Derrick's feeling so bad about Anita relapsing, he continued to beat himself up trying to come to a conclusion about what to do. He moves very quickly, goes to the phone booth dials a number, when someone answers on the other end; Derrick says; yes may I speak to Reverend Franks please? This is he; how may I help you? Hi Reverend Franks this is Derrick. Hi Derrick how are you this fine afternoon? Is everything all right? Yes everything with me is all right, the investigators came to talk to me, and they said it was self-defense. The drug investigators came and searched my car, the apartment and me for drugs, but didn't find anything. That was a stroke of luck, because I usually have some on hand at all times. Rev. the reason I called is because Anita has gotten back on drugs. I've been trying to talk to her, but she want listen to me. That so-called boyfriend of hers is back in town, and somehow he has convinced her that some of the reason for Tim's death was hers. He called her Mother and filled her head with a lot of lies, something about he and Anita was getting back together. Derrick I am so glad you called me thanks. I'll see if I can find her and see what has gotten into her. Okay Rev. she should be in the ally by the store in about an hour. Okay Derrick I'll find her. Rev. you know Tim's funeral is Thursday at 2:00pm. Some of the others and myself are going. We feel like we need to be there for Janice, she's taking it hard. Okay thanks for calling me. I'm going to the funeral also, if anybody needs a ride I'll be glad to pick him or her up. I'm going to find Anita right now, thanks again for calling me. I'll talk to you later.

Reverend Franks goes straight to the south side of town. Once he reach the neighborhood he drives very slow observing every moving thing, not knowing what he's up against once he do find Anita. During his moments of observation he's praying to God to handle this situation before he get to it, then he will just carry it on through. Reverend Franks is now driving down side streets passing the house Anita showed him where she and her little girl's daddy use to hang out, and do their drugs. There were several young men and women loitering around. Reverend Franks slows down wanting to ask them if

Anita was there, but he just drove on by. He turned onto York Street, parked in front of the corner store. He gets, out walks through the path to the ally. Once he entered through the big bushes he sees Anita walking very slow with her head down. Reverend Franks calls out to Anita, she don't look up; but she stops in her tracks, and continues to look down at the ground. Reverend Franks walk up to her; hello! Anita, how are you? Oh Reverend I'm shame; I don't want you to see me like this. Why are you ashamed? What's wrong? Ask Reverend Franks. I'm back on drugs and gonna stay on them; cause I'm a addict. Don't nobody care about me; all they do is tell lies on me and to me. I went to see my mama and baby, mama told me she didn't want my lying self to come back around "them" anymore. And Rev if I hadn't been in the ally talking all that bible stuff, Tim would still be alive. Anita what have gotten into you? Asked Reverend. What make you think like that? Derrick called me earlier; he said he had been trying to talk to you. He said your ex-boyfriend is back in town. Do you know he called your mother? He told her you two are getting back together? Yes Rev. he's back, he's gone to get some more drugs for him and me. He told me he called mama. All he wanted was to see the baby. He said mama went off on him. She can't keep him from seeing his baby, he don changed for the better. But you know Rev. I'm so confused, I guess that's why I just want to stay high and cloud up my problems. When I first saw Randy and told him I didn't do drugs no more. He acted like he was happy for me. That's when he said he wanted to see the baby. When I saw him again he was acting different. When he told me mama wanted to see me, I took for granted he and mama had been communicating and gotten an understanding. When I went to see mama that's when she told me all that stuff. Anita your mother and father don't like Randy because of his ways and the life styles he live; am I right? You right Rev. he's the one that got me hooked on drugs. Mama doesn't like to hear his name, better yet talking to him or see him. Anita you just answered why your mother said what she said to you. Randy said some things to your mother that wasn't true, just to get her upset with you, when he phoned her. He's not going to tell you exactly what he said to her. Then he told you things that would get you upset with yourself. He built you up, then got you to a very low point, then offered you some drugs. He knew what buttons to push to get you there. And you fell right into his trap. Anita you're the only one that can get yourself out of the trap. You know what you have to do. All you're doing now is making excuses and having pity parties with yourself. You're still welcome to come to bible study tomorrow night and the program Sunday. Your family has an invitation also. I will call your family myself and invite them. Anita think real hard about what I said and what you have done. The main thing is what you have worked so hard for and about to give it up okay. Hope to see you tomorrow and Sunday. Are you going to Tim's funeral? No Rev. he wouldn't want me there, because it was just like I killed him. Bringing up that bible stuff, then bringing you around confusing them, that's what Randy said. Anita you listen to me and think about this, that I'm going to say, okay! It was in Gods plan, to take Tim home with him. Tim's duties on earth ended. It was Tim's time to go. There was nothing you or I could have done. Nobody knows when our time is up. Nobody knows the day or the hour. Stop beating yourself up like that, okay. Let me know if you want me to pick you up for the funeral. Derrick and the others are going. Janice would love to see you there she needs all the support she can get, she's taking Tim's death very hard. Think about it okay. Okay Rev. I'll think about it, thanks for coming to fine me. Reverend Franks pats Anita on her shoulder with a very concerned look on his face. Anita I hope you decide to come to church tonight, and tomorrow evening. Derrick and the others are coming. You all need each other now, more than ever. I got to go home and get ready for tonight and tomorrow; can I drop you off anywhere? No Rev thanks anyway, I'm going to hang around here, cause I got a lot to think about. Okay you think and pray he'll help you make the right decision. You have a blessed night, good bye. See ya Rev, said Anita. Reverend Franks goes to his car and drive off.

Anita hangs around pacing back and forth, dealing with the deep thoughts in her mind. She makes her way down the path to the ally. Derrick, Ben, Ali, Kevin and Ron were all sitting around. Anita stops, turns around in a circle looking at everything in sight. Hay what have y'all don? Everything looks so different. Ain't no beer cans or bottles lying around, the old mattress don been moved, the ground is just cleaned up". Derrick says hay Anita! What's up? Nothing says Anita; just decided to come see what you all were up to. We just chilling, sitting around talking says Derrick. We decided to give the ally a face-lift, the ally got to many memories. I ain't never heard the ally this quiet, said Anita. We just sitting here talking about going to Revs church tonight, you going? Asked Derrick. I don't know yet; said Anita. Ron gets up and walks over to Anita, you know Anita the hood don't feel the same to me no more. I ain't never felt this scared in my life, especially here in the hood. I'm scared for all of us. When you left with Randy I was worried to death about you. When Derrick told me what you said about getting high again I wanted to find Randy and beat that nigger down. Then I realized that was your decision. Anita I really don't want to see you go back on the shit"; I really admire the new Anita. Girl! you have been through a lot, and have come a long way. You're a great inspiration for us. We're all we got; you know all of us are stereotyped to be low life anyway, so we all got to stick together, said Ron we family" girl. Anita, Janice needs you now" more than anything; she's got it rough right about now. When I leave here, I'm going straight to her. Where's she? Over at buck's house, Tim's mama doesn't care too much for her being over there. Yall I want y'all to do something for me, and I really mean it okay. Okay what! Asked Ron? Yall know I'm Jonsin, and I don't want to get back out there the way I was. I love being clean and sober. I want yall to help me to stay clean" if you all have to beat my ass okay. Right now I want a rock so bad. Okay Anita all of us will go over Bucks with you okay. Anita starts to crying and hugging all of them, I love all of you. Derrick you gonna miss your customers, said Anita. That ain't important this is, come on yall let's go. On their way through the path Ron speaks up; yo Anita there's Randy! I'll handle this, Anita steps to the front of everybody, walking toward Randy; yall got my back? Hell ya said Ron. Anita where you think you going? Asked Randy. Why? Randy who you think you is? Why you got to talk like that? You ain't my keeper said Anita. Yea but you my bitch, said Randy. Randy you listen to me and listen good. You can say what you want about me, yes I smoked that rock with you today, and I'm paying for it right now, by this guilty and these pity parties I'm having with myself right now. Before you say it, yes Ron and Derrick they dealers, but not mine they're my friends. You're nothing to me but trouble. So Randy leave me the fuck alone, and stay out of my life. Come on yall let's go. Anita heads down the street, everybody else follows her. Randy standing on the street watching his woman walk away, with a surprised and disappointed look on his face. Anita girl, I'm so proud of you said Derrick. Yea! Randy don't know whether to shit or go blind, said Ben. They all laughed and gave each other high five. During the four-block walk to Bucks house, the whole conversation was about Anita's newfound attitude toward Randy.

Look there's Janice sitting in the yard, said Ron. Janice sitting in a single white chair with her arm propped on the chairs arm, her head leaned over resting in her hand. Ron calls out Janice! Janice looks around sees them coming down the street, a big smile comes upon her face. Anita enters the yard first. Janice reaches for her. Anita leans down, they hugs each other very tight. Janice says; girl you're just who I need to see. What you need Janice? Asked Anita. I got it! You're here now. Tim came to me in my dream last night. Girl I had a rough day yesterday, beating myself up about how I should have stopped him from drinking and doing those drugs. My family hates me for sure now. In my dream he told me it wasn't Derricks fault or his. He said it was the spirits fault. Anita what do he mean; the spirits fault? Janice he's talking about that bad spirit that got into him. And the spirits that's in the alcohol and drugs, which caused him to act the way he did. That it was those bad spirits that made him pull that gun and start shooting. You know for yourself that wasn't Tim at that moment. Girl no! That wasn't my Tim; said Janice. You know Anita it's starting to make sense now. So those bad spirits are really out there. Yes mam, in all shapes form and fashions. They never sleep, and they are never off duty; said Anita. Derrick walks up to them, hay yall we gonna split so we can get ready for church. Anita is you going? No Derrick I'll stay here with Janice okay. We're see yall tonight. Okay Derrick thanks for coming by; all of you said Janice. They all said okay and waved good-bye.

When they got to the church, Reverend Franks met them at the end of the isle; he welcomed them with opened arms. Reverend Franks escorted them to some seats, and gave them each a bible and some paper to take notes. He then went to the podium. It was about fifty people in that one class. Looking around the class not seeing nothing but adults, the children were in another part of the church, because every now and then you could hear one from afar. Reverend Franks welcomed everyone, then told them to stand and bow their heads so they could have a word of prayer:

Dear heavenly father, we like to thank you for your son Jesus, heavenly father thank you for our life, health and strength. Lord I want you to touch and fix everyone's heart, soul and mine that is in the sound of my voice. Lord I have the message you have laid on my heart to give out tonight. Lord I'm going to give it in your name. So Lord I'm saying right now that it's well done. Lord open these people's hearts and mine to receive your message, because Lord I feel some hunger for your word in this room. Lord we all give you the praise, we give you the glory, let everybody say a-men.

You may be seated. The subject tonight will be The Two Edge Sword, that will cut in many ways; Mat. 26: 47-54. Class the bible study tonight will be of understanding, confusion and heavy weight off a lot of mines, due to a lot of demon spirits running around on this earth. These spirits they never sleep, they never take brakes, and they're alert at all times. They're just waiting to find the smallest crack that they can crawl in and go to work in your lives. They know when someone has gotten weak in any category. Derrick leans over and whispers to Ali; man Janice said Tim came to her in her dream and told her his death was the spirits fault. Anita told Janice this same thing that Rev talking about now. The goal the evil spirit wants is to hurt you in any kind of way. If it can't go through you it will go through your children, mother, father, sister, brother, friend, co-worker, home, car and etc. I want all of you to turn in your bibles to Matthew 26 chapter. Bible study tonight will come from Matthew 26: 47-54, the arrest of Jesus: I'm going to read these scriptures and give a little input, and then the floor will be open for any questions, and discussions okay. I will be reading from the Good News Translation Bible which is broken down to better understanding, you all can follow alone with me. Verse 47, Jesus was still speaking when Judas one of the Twelve disciples, arrived. With him was a large crowd armed with swords and clubs sent by the chief priest and the elders. Verse 48, the traitor had given the crowd a signal: The man I kiss is the one you want. Arrest him! You see Jesus was still teaching the goodness of the Lord to his disciples when Judas one of his disciples came in with the enemy sent by the chief priest. Judas done sold Jesus out for 30 pieces of silver because the enemy didn't know what Jesus looked like. To identify Jesus to them, he told them the one he kiss is Jesus then they'll know who to arrest. What Judas did was he betrayed Jesus; he sold him out for money. The enemy didn't go to Judas; Judas went to them and asked them. Now if Judas would have been a man of God filled with love what Jesus was teaching them he would have rebuked that evil spirit that approached him, but he let the spirit over power him. Jesus already knew he was going to be betrayed, God had already revealed it to him. Derrick raised his hand. Reverend Franks said yes Derrick; Rev Jesus knew all the time that Judas was going to put the popo on him and Jesus didn't try to hide from the popo? You see Derrick, God had already revealed his plan to Jesus. Jesus didn't want to die. His spirit was willing to die, because of being obedient to his father, but his flesh was weak. Jesus prayed to his father, if this cup of suffering cannot be taken away unless I drink it, your will be done Matthew 26:42. You see Derrick God is a spirit so he couldn't reveal himself to us here on earth, so he planted his seed in woman and produced his son Jesus, so he could walk in his image. He put his son here to prove to us that there is a God. He put his son here to suffer for us. Everything we go through Jesus has experienced it, every pain all of us have had Jesus have had it. God did it for us he gave his only begotten son. Let's read on Verse 49 Judas went straight to Jesus and said, peace be with you teacher, and kissed him. Verse 50. Jesus answered, be quick about it friend. They came up, arrested Jesus, and held him tight. Verse 51. One of those who were with Jesus drew his sword and struck at the high Priest slave, cutting off his ear. Verse 52, Put your sword back in its place "Jesus said to him. All who take the sword will die by the sword. Verse 53, don't you know I could call on my father for help, and at once he would send me more than twelve armies of angels. Verse 54, but in that case, how could the scriptures come true which say that this is what must happen? In verse 49 you see children Judas betrayed Jesus with that kiss, which was a signal to the enemy. That was nothing but that evil spirit at work. That spirit can influence you to have a love one or friend to do something to harm them self and you not even think about it. That spirit can tell you hay this is just having fun. That's why we have to be alert and stay prayed up. Verse 50, Jesus said be quick about it friend, they came up and arrested him, they held him tight. Jesus could have put up a struggle but he didn't because that was in God's plan. Verse 51, one of those who were with Jesus drew his sword and struck at the high priest's slave, cutting off his ear. Verse 52, put your sword back in its place Jesus said to him. All who take the sword will die by the sword. One of the disciples pulled his sword and cut the slave's ear off he did that out of anger trying to defend Jesus. But Jesus told him to put his sword back in its place. All who take the sword will die by the sword. A sword is a two edge-cutting weapon two edges can cut either way. You can determine that in many ways, words can cut through you, for the good or bad, the way you treat your neighbors can cut you in other words things you do to hurt people mentally and physically. Just like in verse 53, Jesus said he could call on his father for help and at once he would send more than twelve armies of angels to help him. If that had been some of us we would have called for help. If Jesus had followed his flesh he would have called for help. Because children our flesh have gotten us in a lot of trouble. Just like in verse 54, but in that case how the scriptures could come true which say, that this is what must happen? Again Jesus is obedient to his father. Jesus is constantly listening to the spirit, when that flesh start troubling him he felled to his knees and prayed to his father. Does anyone have any questions? Derrick raises his hands. Yes Derrick! Rev like with Tim's death, what happens with spirits? Tim believed very much in God. Derrick Tim's flesh got weak, Tim got curious, with the help from his friends to convince him to try those demonic drugs that over powered him. The spirit came at him through himself and his friends. You know sometimes things happen for a reason. Like what happened to Tim, that could wake up a lot of people. Make them look at their lives. Is your life filled with swords? What spirit is your life filled with? Let's take these questions home with us, and next Wednesday we'll pick up from where we stopped. We will stand and dismiss. Everybody stands. Reverend Franks prays: Dear heavenly father again you have aloud us to fellowship together and feed on the goodness of your word. Lord give everyone the understanding of your message tonight. Now Lord as all of us prepare to depart to our destinations for tonight be with us and make sure we arrive safely. Lord this is my prayer in the name of the father, the son and the holy spirit a-men. Every body have a blessed night. Derrick, Ron, Ben, Ali and Kevin they go to the front of the church where Reverend Franks standing. Derrick shakes his hand saying; Rev this bible study was deep it made a lot of sense you answered a lot of confused questions that was in my head. I guess it was questions I can label as feelings to. Rev I want to dig deeper so I can get a better understanding. Is that all right with you? Yes it's all right anytime you're ready son, I'm ready, said Reverend Franks. You all take those bibles with you okay. If you have any questions write them down, so you want forget them. Okay Rev. Thanks again, said Derrick we gonna go now. They all climbed in Derrick's car and goes straight to the ally.

Derrick speaks up; Man I don't like coming to the hood no more since I shot Tim. All I can think about is, that could have been my little brother, or could have been somebody coming after me. I can't even sleep at night. When I close my eyes I can see Tim's face so clear, he keep saying to me, man ain't no future in the life you living. That life is to kill, steal and destroy. That ain't nothing but the spirit of God talking to me in Tim's voice. The stuff Tim was telling us before he died was the spirit of God. Yea man Tim told me that stuff many times. That same day he got shot, he was telling me wasn't no future in using or selling you remember Ali? Yea Tim would get real deep. He said all that stuff is in the bible. Yall think Tim's spirit is right here with us now? Asked Ali. They all starts looking around, if his spirit is here I hope he don't let me see it, said Ben with his eyes stretched big, looking around with a scared look on his face. Man Tim would get real deep with that bible stuff. When I'd turn my forty up it would lose its taste. I'd tell him to gone over there and bother somebody else so I could taste my forty. He would laugh and leave, but man I still couldn't taste my forty, said Ben. Man yesterday I went down to, Wal-Mart and talked to Mr. Collins Tim's boss. He said Tim had talked to him about me. So Derrick man I can't slang no more, my heart want let me. I'm going straight. I go to work this weekend. Ron man we're going straight together, you think they'll give me a job? Hay man go down and see, said Ron. I'll go in the morning. I got to go so I can get myself together for tomorrow. Anybody need a ride? Ask Derrick. No thanks we'll walk. Ron spoke up; Yea man! Will you drop me off? Anita walks out from behind some bushes; Hay Derrick and Ron wait up. Hay Anita what's up? Hay I over heard you all talking about Tim. That's nothing but God sending a message to you all. Tim's death was something for all of us to stop doing harm to our self, our lives and harm to other people. God will plant people and things in your life it's up to you to get the message. Tim's death is making all of us look at our life style. Yea! You right about that cause all I can think about is, if I hadn't been selling drugs, Tim would still be alive today.

Anita, Ron and I are going straight; Ron got him a job at Wal-mart. I'm going tomorrow and try and get me one. We went to bible study at Rev's church. The lesson was about a two edge-cutting sword. The understanding I got from it was me! I'm a two edge cutting sword, because I sale drugs, I teach innocent people how to sale drugs and their bodies, all at the same time they are putting their lives in jeopardy. I was cutting both ways. Hurting people and myself, the more drugs I sold the deeper I was cutting. Every time I think about that, the sicker I feel. If I wasn't a pusher, all this stuff that's going on, tearing every body's world apart in all different areas. Anita you are so right, Tim's death really makes you think of a lot of things, you've never paid any attention to. Derrick that's the Lord dealing with you, be obedient to him okay, said Anita. I'm going back to bible study, because I really enjoyed it. I did to; said Ron. Anita is you going to Tim's funeral tomorrow? Yea Ron I'm not looking forward to it, but I feel like Janice needs all of us at this time. Yes she do, well yall let's go so we can get prepared for tomorrow. They all leave and go home.

CHAPTER NINE

It's 1:00 Thursday afternoon they all agreed to meet in the ally before the funeral, so they could meet Janice at the church. Janice asked them to walk in the church with her and the family. Derrick and the others leaves for the church. When they pulled into the church parking lot, Janice and Robbie is standing on the church steps. They all get out and walk over, and hugs Janice. Janice why are you here? Asked Anita. Why you didn't ride in the family cars? Girl they don't treat me like family. You all are my family. The only family I had is lying in that church dead. He's the only one that claimed me as family. I'm gonna miss him a many days coming. I miss him like crazy right now. I'm dreading going in the church seeing him for the last time, lying in that box. The way I'm feeling now, if Tim was here he knew exactly what to say, to make me feel better. Anita walks up to Janice, puts her arm around her shoulders; Janice Tim's spirit is with you right now. Tim prepared you for this day. Brother Bill walks up and speaks to everybody; how's everybody this afternoon? He hugs Janice and say; Janice I'm so sorry about your lose; God will mend all hearts. Thank you Brother Bill said Janice. He goes on up the steps; opens the church door, the choir's singing Jesus keeps me near the cross. Janice looks at the open door, then looks at Anita: Girl just listen to that song. I don't know if I can go in there. You can do it, do it for Tim okay. Janice you know I got your back, I'm right here beside you. Here come the family cars, come on let's get ready.

The family cars pull in front of the church. Reverend Franks and Reverend Borden come up to the steps. The family gets out; Tim's mother is being helped up the steps, and down the isle by her husband and brother. The music from Lord it's in your hands is being played. Everyone's walking very slowly. All of a sudden an outburst is cried out over the sobbing: Yes Lord I know my baby's there with you, but Lord help me! Tim's mother starts singing Lord it's in your hands. The whole church sympathized with her. The feeling of hearts wanting to help her bare the hurt she was feeling filled the church. The tone from Tim's mother's voice was coming from a very burden down heart. Those tones were touching every heart in the church. Every eye was raining sorrow, identifying with the moment. Seeing this woman being healed, while looking down at her child lying in a coffin knowing that will be the last time she'll ever see him again. Mrs. Miller's husband and brother eased her to her seat on the front row. The rest of the family viewed Tim's body for the last time. Janice walks up to the coffin shaking her head crying out NO! NO! Tim I am so sorry, breaking down into a hard sob. Anita and Derrick grab her before she hit the floor. Janice cries out Mona, I'm so sorry, I should have stopped you. Lord it hurts so bad! I'm so sorry Mona! Derrick puts his arm around Janice's waist helps her to the forth row and sits her down. The rest of the family views the body and sits down. The mortician closes the coffin. Reverend Woods approaches the podium: The reading of the Holy Scripture will be coming from the Old Testament Psalm 26:1-12:

1. Declare me innocent, O Lord, because I do
   what is right and trust you completely.

2. Examine me and test me, Lord; judge my desires and thoughts.

3. Your constant love is my guide; your faithfulness always leads me.

4. 4. I do not keep company with worthless people;
   I have nothing to do with hypocrites.

5. I hate the company of the evil and avoid the wicked.

6. Lord, I wash my hands to show that I am innocent
   and march in worship around your altar.

7. I sing a hymn of thanksgiving and tell of all your wonderful deeds.

8. I love the house where you live, O Lord,
   the place where your glory dwells.

9. Do not destroy me with the sinners; spare
   me from the fate of murderers-

10. Those who do evil all the time and are always ready to take bribes.

11. As for me, I do what is right; be merciful to me and save me!

12. I am safe from all dangers; in the assembly
    of his people I praise the Lord.

Reading of the Holy Scripture New Testament will be read by Reverend

Moore. The Holy Scripture New Testament will be coming from: John 17: 1-8 it reads:

1. After Jesus finished saying this, he looked up to heaven and said, Father, the hour has come. Give glory to your Son, so that the Son may give glory to you.

2. For you gave him authority over all people, so that he might give eternal life to all those you gave him.

3. And eternal life means to know you, the only true God, and to know Jesus Christ, whom you sent.

4. I have shown your glory on earth; I have finished the work you gave me to do.

5. Father! Give me glory in your presence now, the same glory I had with you before the world was made.

6. I have made you known to those you gave me out of the world. They belonged to you, and you gave them to me. They have obeyed your word.

7. And now they know that everything you gave me comes from you.

8. I gave them the message that you gave me and they receive it; they know that it is true that I came from you, and they believe that you sent me.

Prayer of Comfort by Reverend Borden: "Everybody bow your heads and let's go to the Lord in prayer"

Dear heavenly father we come to you with heavy burdened hearts, Lord we know Brother Timothy's there with you, Lord we know he's in a better place now, He's in a place where there is no more pain, there is no more crime, there is nothing but joy. Lord we are selfish, our flesh is mourning for him, Lord I lift this family up to you Lord, Lord help them to deal with the pain and sorrow. Timothy has done what we all has to do. He has paid his debt. His time here on earth was not forever it was borrowed. Lord help this family to understand. Lord we give you the praise, we give you the glory, In Jesus name we pray A-men

Sister Wilma Williams's walks up to the mic, the music fills the church. The recognition of the music was very popular, Precious Lord Take my Hand. When she put the mic to her mouth and sang out Precious Lord! Take my hand-lead me on- the tension from her voice came from deep down within her soul, and soulfully touching every body's hearts. Hands were waving, a-men coming from mouths, yes Lord also filling the church. This moment was very moving. After the beautiful fulfilling solo, the reading of the obituary by Timothy's cousin Gloria Miller followed by remarks:

Timothy Devon Miller, son of Mark and Mona Miller, was born February 15, 1987 in Mission County, Washington DC. He departed this life on May 19, 2003 in the Mission Memorial Hospital Washington DC.

Timothy attended the Public school of Mission County and was a faithful member of Friendship Baptist Church. He was employed with Wal-mart, Main Street, Washington DC, for one and a half years. Timothy loved to talk, that's why he was a people person. He loved to tell about the goodness of God. His presence in his home, work and community will be sorely missed.

Those left to cherish loving memory, his father, Mark D. Miller of the home, his mother Mona H. Miller of the home, one sister, Sherry Lynn Miller of the home, one brother Leonard M. Miller of the home. Grandfathers Timothy Mark Miller, of Washington DC, George L. Hicks of Hampton Virginia. Grandmothers, Valerie H. Miller of Washington DC, Sadie M. Hicks of Hampton Virginia. Aunts, Uncles, a host of cousins, other relatives and dear friends.

The remarks I have to say about this young man lying here before us today are going to be very brief, because the life he lived says it all. He knew no strangers: Timothy we all called him Tim: Speaking for my self and I know I'm speaking for everybody else; I'm feeling a great loss in my life today. I'm going to miss my cousin, my friend, and my teacher. Although I'm four years older than him, I admired him very much. His mind and the life he lived were a lot older than mind. Tim was a wise person. When Tim came into anyone's life, he'd touch very deep, because of his wisdom. He did the work here on earth that God placed him here to do. May 19, 2003, God said Timothy, son Job well done, come on home. Tim left a legacy here with us, which is for, young, middle age, and old people to enjoy the goodness of the Lord, and that God gives us choices on how we live our lives. Tim I know your spirit is right here with us, I to say, job well done and thanks.

Gloria joins her family. Reverend Borden steps up to the podium; Miller family my condolence goes out to each and every one of you. Brother Timothy Miller will be missed in a lot of different areas: Home, school, work, community and here at Friendship Baptist Church. Yes he will be missed. The home going text will come from bits and pieces of the book of Matthew:

the state of mine and the life of Jesus at the moment of these times and those who was with him. In verse 47 Jesus was still speaking to his disciples when Judas one of his twelve disciples arrived with a bunch of men carrying swords and clubs. You see Judas was jealous, and very envious of Jesus he wanted to be in control. In Matthew 26:14 Judas betrayed Jesus he turned Jesus over to the enemy for 30 silver coins. Jesus was put here on earth to save his people from sins. That's what it say in Matthew 1; 21. Jesus knew he was going to be betrayed by Judas, God had already told him Matthew 26:46. Jesus could have ran, he could have hid from Judas, but Judas knew Jesus was obedient to God. That bad spirit had gotten into Judas telling him: Man turn Jesus over to them men and git that money, he don taught you all he know: Now you can be the man. That wasn't anything but the devil. Jesus was suffering with his flesh. His flesh was weak, because he didn't want to die, but his spirit was willing to die like in Matthew 26:39 he prayed for his father to take the suffering from him. It was not what he wanted but what his Father wanted. The reason I'm touching here and there on these scriptures are to get to this: There are evil spirits roaming all over this earth just looking for weak flesh. The Lord put his son here in the flesh to go through different test. Every day of our lives we are tested, but sometimes we all fall by the waist side. But a child God is a forgiver God. The flesh gets curious. Life gets tempting. Temptation creeps in. If we fall short that bad spirit is there to intervene. Bad spirits can come to you in all shapes form and fashions. They can come to you in someone else, like friends and family; that spirit can get into your homes, churches and jobs. We got spirits with names like curiosity, Temptation, Jealousy and envy. Brother Tim was attacked by all of them. These spirits over powered him in his friends as well as in himself. We probably say if things would've been done different; Brother Tim would be here with us today. But brothers and Sisters, God already had everything in his plan. Tomorrow's not promised to any of us. What happened to Brother Tim is a lesson plan for all of us. Just think about it; look at the big picture; if Tim was here right now what would his dos and don'ts be? You can repent from your sinful ways; and God will have mercy on you and forgive you for your sins. His don't is not to live for the devil's doing, the sinful acts the devil wants him to do. His do's is to repent and live religiously and being born again for the Lord. All of us need to take a look at our life styles, because nobody's perfect. Now I will turn everything over to the funeral Director.

The director walks to the podium with some papers in his hand. The Miller family has selected some expressions to share with us as a small token from their heart:

You gave us great Joy

Tim you added great joy to my life each day,

God wanted you so he took you away,

You're one of his angels looking down below,

The love will remain and still forever grow,

Good bye my sweet love, you're now at rest,

I'll miss you dearly, but God knows best.

Forever Yours, Mama and Daddy

Tim we never knew this day would come so soon. You said you wouldn't always be around when we needed you. We wish you were here, but we know you're in a better place than we are. We will miss your smile, your talent and your presence and most of all; we will miss your words of encouragement. We will never forget what you taught us. We love you, your brother and sister

The family would like to present these acknowledgements to you:

Perhaps you sang a lovely song, or sat quietly in a chair;

Perhaps you sent beautiful flowers, if so we saw them there.

Perhaps you sent a card, or spoke kind words as any friend could say;

Perhaps you were not there at all, just thought of us that day.

Perhaps you prepared some tasty food, or maybe furnished a car;

Perhaps you rendered a service unseen, near at hand or from afar.

Whatever you did to console the heart

We thank you so much, whatever the part.

We thank God for each of you and pray that his blessings continually be with you.

The family of the late, Timothy Devon Miller.

As it's stated on your program, the Interment Services will take place at Mission County Memorial Cemetery. Immediately after the interment services, everyone is invited to return to the church to fellowship with the family.

Music starts to play; the director motions for the flower girls and pallbearers to stand. Handing the flowers to the flower girls as they walk slowly down the isle followed by the six pallbearers. As they prepared the coffin to be pushed down the isle constant sniffing and crying came from the family. As the coffin was rolled down the isle the family was motioned to stand and follow it. The six pallbearers were standing three on each side, waiting to assist putting the coffin into the Hurst. The family was placed in the cars to take the heart filled ride to the cemetery. The director told everyone to turn their flashers and headlights on and make sure to keep up with the car in front of them. Just thinking about the ride to the cemetery and the Interment Service was endless pain" said Derrick constantly sharing his thoughts with Ron. Man I feel so full of something that I don't like" man it's in my mind, body and soul; tears streaming down Ron's face, man! I can't hold back my tears said Ron tears raining down his face. This is one ride I don't want to take. Man be strong said Derrick with a very consoling tone of voice, just imaging how Janice is feeling. Derrick man this seem like a bad nightmare, I just want to wake up. Derrick gets real quiet tears rolling down his face, he fighting" looking through the tears to see how to drive. Ben sits up from the back seat, Derrick man" you all right? Yea man! I keep reliving the shooting, the shots keep getting louder and louder, man I can't stop hearing it, what can I do Lord? He breaks down crying, saying over, "I didn't mean to do it", I didn't know it was Tim. Ali sits up; Derrick pulls over and let me drive. Ali man I got it; I'm all right to drive. The cars slow down turning into the cemetery, over the hill the sight of the green tent that covers Tim's final resting place, cars parking along side of the road that leads to it.

Everyone gets out to attend the Interment Service. Ron, Derrick, Ben, Ali and Kevin walk to the tent. Ron standing there looking and saying to himself; this hole dug especially for Tim, where he will sleep eternally, all because I encouraged him to get high for the first time. Tears streaming down his face like the cut off valve had broken off a faucet, and can't be fixed. Janice just sitting under the tent, staring at the coffin as they place it over the grave. Thinking to herself, my favorite nephew lying in that box, knowing she'll never see him again, she'll never hear that sweet voice again. The feeling of loneliness over powering her body, numbness creeping in, affecting her hearing also. Saying to her self-Lord if I could just cry I believe I'd feel better, but my tears has dried up. "This is just a bad dream", "I want to wake up"! She hears some one that sound like they're calling her name echoing in a barrel; Janice! Janice! Are you all right? Seem like everything was echoing in her head. She managed to turn her head and look, she recognizes Anita. She speaks in a soft confused tone; Anita will you wake me up please? Tears rolling down her face. Anita embraced her; wanting to help her bare the pain she was feeling. Janice honey this is not a dream, Anita holding her tight rocking back and forth. Janice come on lets go get in the car it's time to go. Derrick will you help me with her? Anita gently helping Janice to her feet Derrick comes over to help. Derrick and Anita walk Janice to the car. Ron, Kevin, Ben and the girls follows them. They all follows the family to the church, but didn't stay to eat.

They all go back to the ally. Everybody quiet with grief all over his and her face. Derrick, Janice and Ron were sitting on the old sofa staring down at the ground. Derrick jumps up;" man I can't stay here", I got to go! I don't ever want to come back to this ally again. Derrick man I feel the same way; said Ron. Come on everybody let's go to my house said Janice. They all left together.

CHAPTER TEN

A New You

They kept in touch with Reverend Franks. On that following Wednesday night all of them showed up at church accept Anita, Ben and Janice. Saturday evening Reverend Franks had a meeting with the church about the order of service for the program "A New You". He told them the program would be something like they were having the devils funeral; everybody has sinful bones in their body. They went over the outline of the program and dismissed.

At the end of Sunday morning service; Reverend Franks reminded everybody again about the 4:00 program that evening. He told everyone to bring someone with him or her, old and young. Four o'clock that Sunday evening came. The church was over flowing with people, it was standing room only. There were reserved seats up front.

Brother Thomas opened up by saying; lets everybody stand and bow our heads and go to the Lord in prayer:

> Most holy we come to you with bowed down heads, Lord knowing you know each and every ones hearts; Lord you brought us here for a reason; Some of us might have pains in our body; and some of us might just be hungry for your word. Lord touch that burden down heart; Lord touch that paining body; Lord feed that hunger for your word and fix what ever need to be fixed; Lord all of us has congregated here for this A New You program, we know your plan has already been put together, so we know we all will benefit from it; we will say right now Lord job well done. Lord touch the one that put your plan together; Lord touch and stay with the ones that's here in the mix; and when the programs over and we get ready to depart; go with them even if it's next door or way afar make sure they arrive to their destination safe, Lord touch the ones that's here; touch the ones that's not here, and touch the ones that

could be here but just didn't come. Lord we give you the praise and the glory A-men.

Scripture from the Old Testament by Sister Williams

For all of you that have your bibles please turn to Psalms 62 chapter; it reads:

> I wait patiently for God to save me; I depend on him alone. 2. He alone protects and saves me; he is my defender, and I shall never be defeated. 3. How much longer will all of you attack someone who is no stronger than a broken-down fence? 4. You only want to bring him down from his place of honor; you take pleasure in lies you speak words of blessing, but in your heart you curse him. 5. I depend on God alone; I put my hope in him. 6. He alone protects and saves me; he is my defender, and I shall never be defeated. 7. My salvation and honor depend on God; he is my strong protector; he is my shelter. 8. Trust in God at all times, my people. Tell him all your troubles, for he is our refuge. 9. Human beings are all like a puff of breath; great and small alike are worthless. Put them on the scales and they weigh nothing; they are lighter than a mere breath. 10. Don't put your trust in violence; don't hope to gain anything by robbery; even if your riches increase, don't depend on them.

I have read the entire Psalms 62nd Chapter, may the Lord add a blessing to his reading.

The New Testament will be read by Deacon Smith.

Praise the Lord everybody: Everybody that have your bibles if you will turn to Ephesians 2nd Chapter and follow alone with me while I read from the first through the tenth. It reads:

1. In the past you were spiritually dead because of your disobedience and sins.

2. At that time you followed the world's evil way; you obeyed the ruler of the spiritual powers in space, the spirit who now controls the people who disobey God.

3. Actually all of us were like them and lived according to

our natural desires, doing whatever suited the wishes of
our own bodies and minds. In our natural condition we,
like everyone else, were destined to suffer God's anger.

4.   But God's mercy is so abundant, and his love for us is so great,

5.   That while we were spiritually dead in our disobedience he brought
us to life with Christ. It is God's grace that you have been saved.

6.   In our union with Christ Jesus he raised us up with
him to rule with him in the heavenly world.

7.   He did this to demonstrate for all time to come the extraordinary
greatness of his grace in the love he showed us in Christ Jesus.

8.   For it is by God's grace that you have been saved through faith.

9.   It is not the result of your own efforts, but God's
gift, so that no one can boast about it.

10. God has made us what we are, and in our union with
Christ Jesus he has created us for a life of good deeds,
which he has already prepared for us to do.

May the Lord add a blessing to the reading of his word?

Deacon Smith closes his bible, Brother Thomas walk up and joins him
at the front of the church. Good evening everybody; this is another great day
that the Lord has made. It's so good to see all these faces. Some I know and
some I don't know, but we all are God's children. We all are here to lift up the
name of the Lord. So let's join in and give God the highest praises. If anyone
have a song, prayer, or testimony on your heart fill free to do so. I'll start off
with this song: He sings Victory is mine, the congregation joins in. After a few
songs, prayers and testimonies Deacon Smith ends prayer service. Reverend
Franks, Derrick, Brother Bill are standing in front of the church. The usher
tells Reverend Franks that Deacon Smith is introducing the program, A New
You. The usher tells Derrick and Brother Bill the church has seats reserved
for them. Reverend Franks goes in walking very slow meditating and praying.
Brother Bill tells Derrick to tell the other people as they come in because he's
going in to assist Reverend Franks, and help him to win souls.
    Brother Bill walk down the isle of the church hollering; the sky is falling
repent sisters and brothers. Let me lead you to the promise land, come on
church follow me. He is raising his hands, waving his right hand with his

bible in it. Half way up the isle behind him is Sister Lily, Sister Mae and Sister Dot. Sister Mae whispering, "Lord Lily listen at Brother Bill he thank he's God but he ain't doing nothing but making a fool out of himself." Sister Lily gives Sister Mae a look, leans over and tells Mae, shut up there you go talking about people, we in the Lord's house. Sister Dot leans between Sister Lily and Sister Mae and say: Child look like it's a lot of nice looking men in here, but ain't nothing prettier than that man in the pulpit, Reverend John Franks, I'm gonna get that man. Sister Lily tells Sister Dot; you need to shut up, you hotter than a firecracker. You need to sit your tail in some cold water and cool yourself off. Child concentrate on being able to pray a prayer like me. Come on y'all let's go sit down.

Coming down the isle is Brother Bob and Sister Flo; Flo this is a good turnout for the Reverend. You know I helped him to put it together. Bob get on down the isle and shut up lying. There was an usher directing them where to sit.

Coming through the church doors at this time was Ron, Wanda and Shunda. Wanda looking around at everybody in the church, she says in a medium tone of voice to Shunda, "girl, look at all this new money in here! Yea child big money is up in the house!" Said Shunda with a surprised look upon her face, seeing all these people being in one place. Ron walking ahead, Wanda and Shunda stops and look around, Wanda says, "girl I just got to stop and look at all these pretty men and money up in here!" Shunda replies in a higher tone of voice, "yea child! Big money! Big money! Big money!!" Ron stops and hollers down the isle, "yo girls!" Pointing his finger at them, then motions for them to come on, once they get down the isle he points at the seat. Wanda stops before she sits down, she turns looking around at everyone, she hollers out; for as much as I can see, all you men look real good. After services call my beeper: T00-G00D- 866-4663 believe me you want regret it. Ron stands up and says; sit down! Wanda turns and gives Shunda the high five then sits down.

Coming down the isle is Ben and Ali, Ben mumbling, laughing and turning a forty ounce beer bottle up. Ali whispering out loud, "Ben you getting to loud man." Ben continues to walk. Halfway down the isle he stops, looks at his bottle noticing that it's about empty, " Oh snap!" He looks around at the people sitting in the church and walks over to a man sitting at the end of the row, "Hey man, I know you don't know me, but will you do me a favor? Will you run down to that store right down the street, right there" he's pointing his finger telling the man where the store is located, "will you pick me up a forty?" Feeling in his pockets, "Hey, I ain't got no money now, but I'll get you back, I'm good like that." Ali is standing in the middle of the isle restless with an embarrassed look on his face. He walks over to Ben and whispers, "Come on man, that man ain't gonna buy you no beer, you don't need what you got." Ben walks faster down the isle laughing, pointing and yelling, "that's my man!" Ben turns around, points at the man and hollers out, "Hay man! What's your name? Do that for me okay?" Ben and Ali join the others. Ali sits down. Ben walks by Wanda and Shunda stops. He looks down at them and tries to sit saying, "look a here! Look a here!" Shunda speaks, "Ben get your drunk stinky self away from me." Ben sits in the chair down below them on the front row.

Waddling down the isle, Tina, with her big stomach and carrying a baby wrapped in a blanket. She gets half way down the isle stops looks around and says, "Hey, hold up, look like I see some of my baby's daddy's." She sees a man sitting at the end of a row, gives him the baby she's carrying in her arms and say, "here take your baby I got two more at the house and carrying another." She goes over to where the others are sitting and sits down. Ben says, "Girl you big, but still look good." "Old drunk you need to shut up! You couldn't handle this if I gave it to you." replied Tina. Shunda looks at Tina and says, "Don't nobody want a baby factory." "Sister, Child you better shut up, cause I don't want to have to go to you up in here for being with my man. I'll come over there and smack that entire weave out of your head." Wanda jumps up; Ron stands up and snaps his finger and points down. All of them shuts up and sits down. Ben said, as he jumps up going over to Ron, laughing and hollering, with his hand up to give Ron the high five, "Oh snap man you got them under control, I got to give you that." Coming down the isle is Anita and Kevin, Kevin's arm in a sling; he's holding Anita with the other one. Anita's very paranoid, she keep looking around at everybody like she wants to run away. When they get to the end of the isle Ben says; Anita what you scared of girl? Anita and Kevin sit down. Coming down the isle is Janice alone with Robbie walking behind her. She is dressed to kill and walking like she knows she look good. She stops look around and says; what you all staring at? You ain't never seen a beautiful classy woman. She looks back and say, come on baby. They go and sit down. Ben stands up and says; you go girl.

Coming down the isle is Derrick dressed to kill with Dee and Gwen on each arm strolling down the isle. When they get at the end of the isle everybody gives out a hoop and holler.

After everybody is seated the choir begins to sing the opening song of the program. After the opening song the scripture is read coming from Hosea 14th chapter 1-9. Prayer by Deacon Smith. Song by the choir. Deacon Smith introducing the reading of acknowledgment by Sister Mary.

This program was put together to let everyone know how evil spirits can arrive into our lives and the different roles they make us play which is of the devil. Here is how these evil spirits and Demons got here on earth.

The Devil known as Lucifer, Satan and Beelzebub was created by God and placed at the head of all the angels. He was very beautiful and worked alone side of God. He put some of the angels up to revolt against God. In punishment for his disobedient God cast him out of heaven alone with him was the other disobedient angels, which were transformed into demons. As ruler over the fallen angels from now on, Lucifer continues to fight against the kingdom of God in three ways:

1. He seeks to seduce man into sin:

2. He tries to disrupt God's plan for salvation:

3. And he appears before God as slander and accuser of the saints so as to reduce the number of those chosen for the kingdom of God.

The devil has had a good time working in your homes, churches, jobs and mainly in your life. The devil knows he can live on in you but today you can bury him and gather the armor of God to shield you from him. The devil is survived by his wife (Jez'ebel) family of Addicts, Drunks, Pregnant Unmarried Ladies and Men, Adulterers, Hypocrites, False Prophets, Murders, Drug Dealers, Liars and a host of others. An up lifting song was sung by the choir. After the song Reverend Franks walks up to the pulpit. He places the mic in the position that he wants it, he clears his throat then he speaks: First of all I would like to give God the highest praise, and to thank him for his son Jesus. I would like to thank all of you for coming out this evening to taste of this spiritual food that God is about to place before you. Right now I would like for everyone to stand and join hands with your neighbor while we go to God in prayer.

Dear heavenly father I come to you with my heart opened, Lord fill my heart with what you know it need, Lord I want to be just like you, My heart, my mind and soul. Lord I have standing here with joined hands, is your children. Lord start a chain reaction of wisdom, start a chain reaction of faith, Lord start a chain reaction of trust. Lord you know what each and everyone of them is in need of, Lord you know what each and every one of them is missing. Lord you know every body's needs in this whole wide world. Lord touch me Jesus, strengthen me in your word. Lord this program today is yours, yes Lord you can use my body, you can use my mind, Lord you can use my soul, Lord you can use whatever you want. This is my prayer to you Lord A-men.

Brothers and Sisters, I come to you to tell you life can be a confusing thing. Life can deal you a hand that you don't know what to do with. Once you start trying to figure out how to play that hand a voice will say go head play that one, if you lose you can always build another one. But in your mind you want to win, you want to gain victory. Victory is happiness; proud, positive, most of all it helps to keep the morals in the individual built up, to better ones self. Children always reach for victory. Victory is love, victory is God. God loves to see us win. The devil loves to see us lose. We have two choices: 1. to win: or 2.To lose: to win is the voice of God telling you to always give everything you do, your very best. To lose is the voice of the devil telling you to always settle for less. Losing can cost you to feel deeper and deeper in the dumps. Once you get so deep you come to the conclusion that you don't care, pity parties set in, the devil starts rejoicing and saying, ok I bout got them, now go drank that alcohol, go do that dope, go sale that evil drug, pimp that innocent child. The devil will plant negative things in your head if you allow him or her. Everybody's just out to hurt you, they ain't doing nothing but trying to use you. God done forgot about you. There ain't no God. You can do whatever you want yourself. You can control God's plan. Go ahead on lie and get what you want. God put all those men out there for you see how many you can get. Ain't nothing wrong with gossiping, boasting and bragging. Don't let nobody talk that junk to you, that makes you a chicken, shoot that person. Go head try a little alcohol and drug ain't nothing wrong with it. Once you have reacted to the devil's subjections it adds more negative clutter to your mind. As the clutter grows the deeper in the dumps you get. My reason for touching on these few things it leads me to the book of Hosea: Idolatry of the people and their faithlessness toward God. You see children God works mysteriously. Everything God allows to happen it's for a reason. Sometimes when we get impatient and act hasty, God will get our attention: How many of us have asked this question? Why God? God has his way of slowing us down, sitting us still or laying us on our back, even taking a love one to get us to look at our self about the life we live. It's up to us to stand still and recognize. That's when our choices come in, remember, God is not selfish, it's up to you, to be obedient to God.

Let's turn our bibles to the book of Hosea 1st chapter 2nd verse: When the Lord first spoke to Israel through Hosea, he said to Hosea, Go and get married, she will be unfaithful, and your children will be just like her, In the same way my people have left me and became unfaithful. You see God had a plan for his people of Israel, so he spoke to his prophet Hosea, who has been searching for him a wife, going from church to church looking high and low. God told him to go on the block, to the Red Light and find his wife, which was a low section of town. He did what God said. Time he laid eyes on Gomer the prostitute he knew he loved her. God told him to marry that unfaithful woman. You know it crossed Hosea's mind, why do the Lord want me to marry that woman, knowing she's going to cheat on me? Okay Lord I'll marry her. Hosea was especially concerned about the idolatry of the people and their faithlessness toward God. He pictured the unfaithfulness in terms of his own disastrous marriage to an unfaithful woman. Just as his wife Gomer turned out to be unfaithful to him, so God's people had deserted the Lord. Hosea was very obedient to the Lord. He was the prophet; God chose him to get his message out. God is a spirit; he can't appear here in front of us and tell us what he wants from us. He's always with us. He's constantly telling us the right things to do it's up to us to be patient and listen to him. Hosea married the unfaithful woman, knowing the message God had given him. That's being obedient, having faith and trusting in God's word. God went to the bottom of the barrel and pulled this one out. In other words God is letting us know, all of us is his children. He don't love one no more than the other. This woman is a prostitute, but God knows her heart, God has plans for her, just like he has plans for Israel. Both of these task are similar, the unfaithfulness. Being unfaithful in any kind of way, we fill that's the easy way out, satisfying the flesh, but being faithful and meaning it from the heart is like money in the bank because the blessings from God will pour in. You know a lot of people think in order to get a job done right, you have to go get a college graduate that's well educated, living in a rich neighborhood, driving a big expensive cars, wearing name brand cloths. God chose a prostitute, someone that loves selling her body for money, wine, grain and goods to dress in, someone that's being a shameless prostitute. This woman putting idols before God, she was using her body, her flesh to get what she wanted. God will plant people in your life to give you his message; it's up to you to be obedient. That's what Hosea is doing being obedient to God, being a message carrier to Gomer and Israel.

In Hosea chapter 2: 6-7 God said speaking to Hosea: 6.So I am going to fence her in with thorn bushes and build a wall to block her way. 7. She will run after her lovers, but will not catch them. She will look for them but will not find them. Then she will say, I am going back to my first husband, I was better off than I am now. God fixed it to where things went bad for Gomer, so she came back home to her husband, that's where God wanted her to be. Whatever go wrong in life, God is right there with you at all times. The solution to fix it is right there, it's up to you to be patient, and let God handle it for you.

In the book of Hosea 4th chapter verse 1-3: God was very displeased with Israel. The prophet Hosea preached in the Kingdom of Israel he was concerned about the idolatry of the people. Hosea figured, God being displeased with Israel was connected with him being displeased with his unfaithful wife. Let's go to our bibles: Hosea 4th chapter verse 1-3 it reads: 1.The Lord has an accusation to bring against the people who live in this land. Listen Israel, to what he says: There is no faithfulness or love in the land, and the people do not acknowledge me as God. 2. They make promises and break them; they lie, murder, steal, and commit adultery. Crimes increase, and there is one murder after another. 3. And so the land will dry up, and everything that lives on it will die. All the animals and birds, and even the fish will die. Accusation means: Blame, to change, accused, accusal and marking the direct object. God brought the children out of Egypt. They have showed no appreciation to what God has done for them. They don't show no faithfulness or love in the land. Since they have gotten to Israel they act like God don't exist. They promise they are going to worship God, then go off and do other thing that's more important to them. They tell lies of all kind, get drunk, act crazy, murder, steal and commit adultery. A lot of us don't think about God until we are in trouble or sick. Children, God is selfish he want recognition at all times, during good and bad times. The children of Israel was making idol Gods and worshiping them. Like in Hosea 4th chapter verse 4: Let no one accuse the people or reprimand them-my complaint is against you priest. Verse 5: Night and day you blunder on, and the prophets do no better than you. Children just like in the acknowledgement Sister Mary read, there are mischief bad spirits roaming around this earth right now, with all different titles; Just like in verse 4: The people was misled by the priest, which is called a false prophet. Spirits of a false prophet Mat. 7th chapter 15th verse and Jer. 23th chapter 16-21 verse wants to control Gods plan. He wants people to follow him and believe in him like he's God, and tell people the untruth. A person like that is dangerous; they are like a wolf in sheep clothing. Children beware of a false prophet. Israel had some people call hypocrites: Spirits of a hypocrite: Mat. 6th chapter 2-5th verse hypocrite is a person that boast and brag about anything they do. They think nobody else can do nothing better than they can. They do something for someone, then go around and broadcast it all around town. Children beware of a hypocrite. Israel had a lot of liars; Spirits of Liars James 3rd chapter 14th verse are dangerous people, they will sin against the truth, you can't believe nothing they say. They will lie to cover up a lie; they will even lie to their love ones. Just remember a liar has to have a good memory, but pretty soon you will forget. So the best thing to do is not to lie. Be very cautious of a liar. Spirits of Backbiters: Roman 1st chapter verse 30 a backbiter is a person, all up in other people's lives speaking

evil of one and another. They are hateful to God. They think of more ways
to do evil. Wanting to control and spread other people's business trying to
get things in their favor, they also disobey their parents, in other words they
are good friends with a liar, in street terminology a drama queen or king, a
control freak. They are miscible people that don't know how to handle their
own life, so they choose to try and control others. This act is sneak work of
the devil, and they love to be superior and gain company. Another sneak
evil roll is a spirits of adulterers 1st Cor. 6th chapter 9th verse children don't
fool your selves; people who are immoral or who worship idols are adulterers
or homosexual perverts. They are wicked, greedy, unhappy and love to find
someone to join them in their miserable life. An adulterer loves to invade
people's marriage, mind, home and lives. An adulterer is very seductive and
wants to cause confusion, so beware of an adulterer. Spirits of prostitutes Col.
2:22 and Rom. 6:5-8 Children using your bodies to get what you want is not
of God. You become useless once you are used. Just like they were doing in
Israel and the way Hosea's wife Gomer a shameless prostitute. Please beware
of a shameless prostitute. Spirits of Drunks Eph. 5:18 is an evil and can be an
abusive spirit beyond the individual's control. This spirit is very controlling.
So do not get drunk with wine, which will only ruin you; instead, be filled
with the Spirit. Spirits of unmarried pregnant young ladies and unmarried
young men, children don't misuse your bodies in the act of lust, surely you
know that the wicked will not possess God's Kingdom. Use your bodies for
God's glory. Spirits of Young murder and Drug dealers Gal. 5:19-21 and
Spirits of Drug dealers and Pimps Jer.17:9-11 these evil acts are immoral,
filthy and indecent actions. Selling that demonic drug to people, that do
bodily harm to them self and causing harm to others mentally and physically.
Taking lives of others probably because of the sale of the drug or pimping in
other words selling of ones wife or daughter. This act can be called worship
of idols and witchcraft. Causing people to become enemies and they fight;
they become jealous, angry and ambitious. People who do these things will
not possess the kingdom of God. I would like to read Jeremiah 17th chapter
9-11 verse it reads:

Who can understand the human heart?

There is nothing else so deceitful;

It is too sick to be healed.

I the Lord, search the minds

And test the hearts of people.

I treat each of them according to the way they live,

According to what they do.

The person who gets money dishonestly

Is like a bird that hatches eggs it didn't lay

In the prime of life he will lose his riches,

And in the end he is nothing but a fool.

The reason for reading this to you is because these scriptures I have just read, it says a lot about life's walk in the light of God. These verses's says a lot to get rid of all the evil spirits I just spoke about. Sisters and Brothers this box that I have here is a coffin that we can bury all our sins. I want you to think about the message that God gave me to deliver to you tonight. I want you to come up and look in the box and bury those spirits that you have within you. The choir starts singing. Ushers comes forth opens the small box. I want all of you to take time while the choir sings to think about the sermon God laid on my heart to preach to you tonight. Think about the life you live. Are you proud of the life you live? Come on choir sing your song. Come on children think, think about yesterday think about your life on that day when some of you all's best friend got shot and killed why? Because he tried something against his will. Think about the evil spirit that runs through one's body when they puff on that pipe that's filled with crack cocaine, think about that evil spirit in that powdered cocaine that's sniffed up the nose. The evil tobacco that they roll those joints and blunts out of. That evil spirit that makes you drink that beer, liquor and wine until it controls you. Those evil spirits that make you lie to love ones and everybody else, but you can't lie to God. God knows you tell one lie to cover up another lie. That evil spirit that makes you hurt people mentally and physically. That evil spirit that makes you talk about people, that make you gossip. That evil spirit that makes you boasts and brags about yourself. That evil spirit that makes you try to control God's plan. That evil spirit that makes you sale your body for money. That evil spirit that makes you bring children in this world and you don't want to take care of them. Children just think, is God pleased with that?

While the music plays children I want you to come up and look into this box. Once you look into it leave all those sinful spirits of evil ways in it and let's bury them and become A New You. Let's start from the back of the church, come on children. As the people were coming around viewing the box, Reverend Franks was walking around talking to people. After the viewing of the box Reverend Franks announces; sisters and brothers Ali has something he would like to share with us. Ali walks up to the podium

I want to say thank you God and thank you Reverend Franks. Reverend Franks meeting you was the best thing that could happen to me. That old saying God works in mysterious ways, that is very much true. Because that ladies car stopping on her and all those people trying to fix it even a licensed mechanic couldn't find the problem. That was an act of God for me to come alone and show my mechanical skills about fixing cars. Reverend Franks no one ever had faith in me. People have always put me down. When you told me to never let anyone steal my joy, to always believe in God and myself, it works. Every since that day my faith have gotten stronger and this song can explain it all. Ali starts singing I believe I can fly. The choir helps him out. After the song Reverend Franks walks back to the podium; Ali yes God might not come when you want him but he is right on time. God sends us messages, it is up to us to accept them, if we don't it will pass right by us. Sisters and Brothers having you to look in this box was a way I thought of to get my message across to you. You can bury your sins and become new. Now is just as good as anytime. Just talk to God and mean it from your heart and become "A New You."